JO

JOSEPH

Eleven Bible Studies on Genesis

Claus Westermann

Translated by Omar Kaste

FORTRESS PRESS   MINNEAPOLIS

JOSEPH
Eleven Bible Studies on Genesis

First English-language edition published 1996 by Fortress Press.

This book is a translation of *Die Joseph-Erzählung: Elf Bibelarbeiten zu Genesis 37–50*, by Claus Westermann. Published 1990 by Calwer Verlag. German original copyright © 1990 by Calwer Verlag Stuttgart.

Library of Congress Cataloging-in-Publication Data

Westermann, Claus.
   [Joseph-Erzählung. English]
   Joseph : eleven Bible studies on Genesis / Claus Westermann : translated by Omar Kaste. -- 1st English-language ed.
     p. cm.
   Includes bibliographical references (p.).
   ISBN 0-8006-2583-8 (alk. paper)
   1. Bible. O.T. Genesis XXXVII, 1-L, 26--Criticism, interpretation, etc. 2. Joseph (Son of Jacob) I. Title.
BS1235.2.W453413 1996
222'.1106--dc20   95-49273
                                               CIP

1–2583

00   99   98   97   96   1   2   3   4   5   6   7   8   9   10

Contents

Introduction

Few stories in the Bible tell of God's interaction with the people as intimately and humanly as does the story of Joseph. The careful reader is rewarded with a sense of real familiarity with the events in the lives of this small circle of human characters. Time and time again, one is struck by the fact that most of the circumstances in this story could just as easily have taken place in our own modern day. So much in this tale seems so familiar that it hardly seems appropriate to categorize it as some sort of time capsule from a distant time and place.

As to the story's scope, it follows a particular progression from the smallest social unit to the very largest, then back again. In the beginning, the scene is narrow, limited to a single family; the scene then gradually widens until it eventually encompasses the entire body politic; finally, as events run their course, the scene again narrows its focus on just the family.

The basic plot is easily summarized. A father favors one son over all the others, and this favoritism sparks ill-will in the ones who feel slighted, which in turn leads to wrongdoing and undeserved suffering. But there is one among the jealous brothers who feels a strong sense of responsibility. Finally, following one confusing turn of events after another, the one truly important thing becomes an old man's desire to die in peace.

By no fault of its own, the family becomes enveloped by the kind of catastrophic famine that is as common in our day as it was in theirs. The fate of the smallest social unit, the family, is thus inextricably bound to the fate of the whole world. Family members suddenly find themselves at the mercy of the powerful; an ordinary man finds himself tossed into prison without regard for the fact that he happens to be innocent. As is the case today, the starving have no choice but to throw themselves at the feet of those who have plenty, and humbly to acquiesce when they are unjustly abused.

Beneath this surface story of power and politics, there are the underlying themes of guilt and punishment, then guilt and forgiveness – all of this accompanied by the wrenching apart and subsequent healing of the family unit.

The ending, too, is rather unusual: one of these little people, fugitives from poverty, takes it upon himself to bestow his blessing on the grand and powerful Pharaoh! And, in the end, there is also the behind-the-scenes presence of one whose hand guides every event, small or large, from beginning to end.

For each specific interpretation of the biblical text offered here it would be helpful for the reader to follow the text of the NRSV or the RSV.

The Origins of the Story of Joseph

Chapters 37–50 of Genesis tell the story of one family, but this story actually belongs to the larger story of the patriarchs which are found in chapters 12–36. The story itself begins with the antagonism between the brothers and ends with their reconciliation and Joseph's reunion with his father. The following chapters (46–50) constitute the conclusion of the story of Joseph, and are closely related to chapters 25–36.

The story of Joseph, strictly speaking, is found in chapter 37 and chapters 39–45. These passages form a tightly-knit and homogeneous narrative. Its beginning in chapter 37 is related to sections of the story of Jacob, which reveals an intertwining of two narrative threads (in the names, for example).

Chapter 37 and chapters 46–50 constitute the conclusion to the story of Jacob, relating how he and his family came to Egypt, and it is into this conclusion of the Jacob story that the story of Joseph (chapters 37–45) is fitted. The two stories evolved independently, and were skillfully woven together later. This combination from two sources explains, for example, why the words of interpretation in 45:5–8 are repeated in 50:17–21.

The Biblical Context of the Story

Thematically, the story of Joseph is a constituent part of the stories of the patriarchs, which span Genesis 12 through 50. Geographically, these stories are all limited to the domains occupied by the family or tribe, and they hark back to an era when social life existed exclusively on the level of family. The stories of the patriarchs preserve the memory of a *pre*-political epoch. This is true also – sometimes primarily so – of the kind of interaction between God and human being that occurs in these stories; everything happens inside the boundaries of kin, and everything contributes in some way to the life and perpetuation of the extended family: the birth of a child; the endangerment and preservation of the mother; the plight of childlessness, as well as the miraculous deliverance from it; rivalry between the first wife and the second; conflict between brothers; the birthright of the firstborn and loss thereof; the blessing of the father and the securing of a bride for the son. In these stories, all these events are intimately bound up with God's work, God's instructions and promises, God's gifts as well as the withholding of gifts, and God's words as well as silences. Thus, the theological perspective of all these stories cannot be isolated from the form of the community in which these things take place.

Within the cycle of the stories of the patriarchs, the story of Joseph is the last, which means that it represents the transition from family history to national history. It also represents the moment in which the family widens its scope and exposes itself to the larger world. There is much evidence of this state of transition between family history and national history in the story of Joseph, but the primary evidence is the recurrent preoccupation with the problem of political authority and, more specifically, the fundamental problem of royal authority: How is it that a man can lord it over his own brothers? Joseph's dreams deal with precisely this problem, among other things. And yet the story of Joseph reflects even more intensely the historical moment in which the heretofore self-contained extended family begins to make contact with the external world and opens itself up to that world. Time and again, we are struck by the family's sense of awe as they encounter a superior culture with the economic and political institutions of a world-class empire, as well as the powerful and violent individuals who inhabit it. Their sense of awe is the reflection of a historical experience: the crossing of the threshold from the old mode of existence to the new. The old mode of existence was defined in its totality by life inside the wandering tribe, the necessities of this life, and the tribe's relationship with a guiding and protecting God. Now a whole different set of factors has come into play, delivering them into the new mode of existence – that of a growing nation. Thus, one must understand that it is precisely this transition *out* of the old mode which calls attention *to* the old mode; this is to say, the past experiences of God's active will inside the old family order are now remembered, and transformed into a story-form that is the perfect vehicle for passing the memory of these experiences of God on to the latter generations of the new order.

Yet, if the purpose here is to accurately locate in the biblical context the story of Joseph, then the above explanation is incomplete. For this story, the story of the end of the era of patriarchs and of the transformation of a small tribe into a nation engaged with the larger world, is told from the perspective of an era that came much later – the reigns of David and Solomon. It must be made clear that we are not dealing here with a historical account that was written according to our own modern definition of "historical"; the story's main purpose is to describe the end of the era of patriarchs from the point of view of a later epoch. The influence of this latter perspective notwithstanding, it is still possible to discern clear traces of a preexistent foundation that reaches back to the era of the patriarchs.

The Structure of the Story of Joseph

The story is structured by means of its two locales: the home of Jacob and the Egyptian court. The story leads from the threatened break between the sons of Jacob (chapter 37) to the healing of the family bonds (chapter 45), which is made possible by Joseph's elevation to authority in the Egyptian court. There are really two separate story lines: chapters 39–41, describing Joseph's ascent to power, and chapters 42–45, which recount the brothers' journeys and eventually leads to the unification of the two story lines.

This arrangement, with the two story lines and the tension that gradually builds as the brothers must travel back and forth, shows the handiwork of a poet. The two-membered structure of the story reflects the two sides of the history of the people of Israel – the time of the patriarchs and the time of kings. The question raised is that of the kingdom's relationship to the old order of an earlier time. (The story most likely originated during the reigns of David and Solomon.)

1

The Peace is Shattered in Jacob's Family (Genesis 37)

Text

37 *Jacob settled in the land where his father had lived as an alien, the land of Canaan. ²This is the story of the family of Jacob.*

Joseph, being seventeen years old, was shepherding the flock with his brothers; he was a helper to the sons of Bilhah and Zilpah, his father's wives; and Joseph brought a bad report of them to their father. ³Now Israel loved Joseph more than any other of his children, because he was the son of his old age; and he had made him a long robe with sleeves. ⁴But when his brothers saw that their father loved him more than all his brothers, they hated him, and could not speak peaceably to him.

5 Once Joseph had a dream, and when he told it to his brothers, they hated him even more. ⁶He said to them, "Listen to this dream that I dreamed. ⁷There we were, binding sheaves in the field. Suddenly my sheaf rose and stood upright; then your sheaves gathered around it, and bowed down to my sheaf." ⁸His brothers said to him, "Are you indeed to reign over us? Are you indeed to have dominion over us?" So they hated him even more because of his dreams and his words.

9 He had another dream, and told it to his brothers, saying, "Look, I have had another dream: the sun, the moon, and eleven stars were bowing down to me." ¹⁰But when he told it to his father and to his brothers, his father rebuked him, and said to him, "What kind of dream is this that you have had? Shall we indeed come, I and your mother and your brothers, and bow to the ground before you?" ¹¹So his brothers were jealous of him, but his father kept the matter in mind.

12 Now his brothers went to pasture their father's flock near Shechem. ¹³And Israel said to Joseph, "Are not your brothers pasturing the flock at Shechem? Come, I will send you to them."

He answered, "Here I am." [14]So he said to him, "Go now, see if it is well with your brothers and with the flock; and bring word back to me." So he sent him from the valley of Hebron.

He came to Shechem, [15]and a man found him wandering in the fields; the man asked him, "What are you seeking?" [16]"I am seeking my brothers," he said; "tell me, please, where they are pasturing the flock." [17]The man said, "They have gone away, for I heard them say, 'Let us go to Dothan.'" So Joseph went after his brothers, and found them at Dothan. [18]They saw him from a distance, and before he came near to them, they conspired to kill him. [19]They said to one another, "Here comes this dreamer. [20]Come now, let us kill him and throw him into one of the pits; then we shall say that a wild animal has devoured him, and we shall see what will become of his dreams." [21]But when Reuben heard it, he delivered him out of their hands, saying, "Let us not take his life." [22]Reuben said to them, "Shed no blood; throw him into this pit here in the wilderness, but lay no hand on him" – that he might rescue him out of their hand and restore him to his father. [23]So when Joseph came to his brothers, they stripped him of his robe, the long robe with sleeves[d] that he wore; [24]and they took him and threw him into a pit. The pit was empty; there was no water in it.

25 Then they sat down to eat; and looking up they saw a caravan of Ishmaelites coming from Gilead, with their camels carrying gum, balm, and resin, on their way to carry it down to Egypt. [26]Then Judah said to his brothers, "What profit is it if we kill our brother and conceal his blood? [27]Come, let us sell him to the Ishmaelites, and not lay our hands on him, for he is our brother, our own flesh." And his brothers agreed. [28]When some Midianite traders passed by, they drew Joseph up, lifting him out of the pit, and sold him to the Ishmaelites for twenty pieces of silver. And they took Joseph to Egypt.

29 When Reuben returned to the pit and saw that Joseph was not in the pit, he tore his clothes. [30]He returned to his brothers, and said, "The boy is gone; and I, where can I turn?" [31]Then they took Joseph's robe, slaughtered a goat, and dipped the robe in the blood. [32]They had the long robe with sleeves taken to their father, and they said, "This we have found; see now whether it is your son's robe or not." [33]He recognized it, and said, "It is my son's robe! A wild animal has devoured him; Joseph is without doubt torn to pieces." [34]Then Jacob tore his garments, and put sackcloth on his loins, and mourned for his son many days. [35]All his sons and all his daughters sought to comfort him; but he refused to be comforted, and said, "No, I shall go down to Sheol to my son, mourning." Thus his father bewailed him. [36]Meanwhile the Midianites had sold him in Egypt to Potiphar, one of Pharaoh's officials, the captain of the guard.

Structure

In summary, this is the course of the narrative in chapter 37:

3–4	The father's favoritism and its consequences
5–11	Joseph's dreams
12–30	The brothers' removal of Joseph from the scene
31–35	The father's grief

Chapter 37 contains ample evidence of the two separate storylines that were combined in the story of Joseph. In fact, it is possible to reconstruct from chapter 37 two separate and complete descriptions of the conflict within Jacob's family and the subsequent selling of Joseph into slavery. Let it be understood from the beginning that it is completely appropriate to present chapter 37 in its final form when reading it before the congregation. However, whoever proposes to teach it must be familiar with the history of its formation so that he or she may know how to distinguish between the two distinct voices that are joined in it and to be aware of their respective contributions to the whole.

Interpretation

Verses 1–2 belong to the "Priestly document" (P). Verse 1 is the conclusion to the story of Jacob as well as the segue into the story of Joseph. Verse 2 is a separate, independent introduction to an account of the rift that formed between Joseph and his brothers. It contains its own explanation, namely, that Joseph had informed his father of what was being said about the sons of Bilhah and Zilpah. Apparently P wants to portray the family conflict as an event limited to the sons of the maids. This is typical of this editor's tendency to shield the patriarchs and try to keep their reputations as spotless as possible. The fact that Joseph tells Jacob of the circulating rumors is merely intended to illustrate the loyal bonds between father and son.

Here, however, P's account breaks off, and there is no further development. These two verses serve to lend a priestly introduction to chapters 37–50, in the same way that words from P frame many other major portions of the Pentateuch.

37:3–4 *The Father's favoritism and its consequences*

The very first phrase, "Now Israel loved Joseph more than any other of his children," raises the issue of what we have come to call Jacob's "favoritism" (*Vorliebe*). This favoritism is explained by saying that Joseph was the son of Jacob's old age. This may seem very commonplace to us – all part of the day-to-day of human existence – and the reader is likely to regard Jacob's preference of one son as wholly unremarkable. However, this seemingly commonplace and insignificant event has been positioned as the opening of a grand, dramatic tale. In other words, the storyteller recognized the deeper meaning of this man's preference for the child of his old age and turned what was just an isolated phenomenon into a link in a chain of wider events; thus the smaller event gains significance from the story's larger structure of meaning. This interpretation presupposes that the storyteller was consciously trying to recreate a distant time in which the experience of family and clan had been central, as opposed to his own politically and nationally oriented era.

In the world of the patriarchs, not only is a father's favoritism of greater significance but it also takes on greater clarity. The old man is approaching his death. He is aware of this in a way that would be impossible for a man at the height of his powers or a young man to imagine. He is nearing the very end. To have a child born to him at precisely this moment, as his life's force is ebbing away, is fundamentally different from becoming a father when he was young and strong. The generational gap between begetter and begotten is heightened. The child, by the simple fact of being a child, constantly seems to say to his elder, "I will still be here when you are gone." Because this situation is so special, the relationship between an aged father and the child born in his old age must also be special – and different. As Gunkel says, while we would see this favoritism as an injustice, the old Israelite would reply that

no one can love two children equally. The story is trying to
show us that the relationship between parent and child can
be unique, simply the result of its unique situation. When
the storyteller says that Jacob "loved Joseph more than any
other of his children," the comparative form is merely an
approximation of the truth, as is our understanding of this
kind of favoritism. This is not just an intensification of love,
but an indicator of a relationship between two people whose
special nature cannot be expressed adequately in words.
Thus, if we try to apply our own moral yardsticks to judge
Jacob's favoritism, we will end up misinterpreting this story
from the very outset. The storyteller's perspective of Jacob's
favoritism is utterly free of criticism; his intention is to
present it merely as one special – and fateful – instance in
human relations. He reveals it precisely in its
meaningfulness as a special and fateful phenomenon of
human nature. So, too, should we understand it.

"And he had made him a long robe with sleeves." The
story's conflict is born when the special relationship
between Jacob and the child of his old age is expressed in a
concrete action. Jacob's preference for Joseph is simply a
matter of fact, and should not be seen here as a fault.
Furthermore, it cannot simply be said that the giving of the
gift was wrong, for love, by its nature, always seeks to
express itself in concrete actions. Instead, the fault should
be located in the fact that Jacob's special love for Joseph is
openly proclaimed in the form of this gift. The gift, which
acts as a document of Jacob's favoritism, sparks an incident
for which everyone, including Jacob, shares some portion
of guilt. It is the storyteller's purpose to point out exactly
this. This action by which they then all come to share guilt
cannot simply be blamed on the error of any single person;
the incident is somehow self-powered, because no matter
how we try to assign blame, some of it always remains
unallocated. The things that happen here are as
fundamentally inexplicable as the events described in
Genesis 3. Out of the love of a father for his son springs an
event that leads first to the loss of equilibrium and then to
the shattering of the peace of the family.

In the Septuagint the Hebrew *ketonat passim* (many-
colored coat) is translated as "multi-colored robe," as is the
case in the Latin and the Luther Bible. Gunkel, along with

the majority of scholars, prefers the translation "long robe with sleeves." The actual meaning of the original Hebrew is not known with entire certainty. However, since in 2 Samuel 13:18 the same expression is used to describe the attire of a princess, we can conclude that the garment in question is rather distinctive. Thus, it is safe to assume that Jacob was doing more than simply giving Joseph a nice gift; he was raising the boy to a level above that of his brothers. Here we must keep in mind the social function of clothing, which throughout the millennia has been one of the strongest and most conspicuous indexes of social status. Only in our own day and age has clothing come to lose some of this emblematic significance, and this is only because of the deep-rooted changes in human society which have been taking place of late.

The robe, the gift that is the fruit of the father's favoritism, plays a role in this story which could hardly be possible for any piece of clothing today; nonetheless, in our world, similar tokens of favoritism have cost many tears and caused much blood to be spilled.

Verse 4. "His brothers saw that their father loved him more than all his brothers . . ." Here we have it spelled out for us: the events of this story are ignited when Jacob takes the small step from preference to partiality. In the act of setting one son apart, the father's favoritism comes to the surface for all to see. At this moment, in which a preference becomes an action, which in turn leads to an event which is seen by others, we begin to have a story in the broadest sense of the word. And this is how a special love finally disturbs and threatens the very structure of the community.

This passage is a good example of the general narrative style of the entire Old Testament. Everything that happens in OT stories must happen in a live forum, in contrast with the Western narrative style of the eighteenth and nineteenth centuries, in which events that are central to a story take place in the arena of private thoughts and feelings. The people who wrote and acted in the stories of the Old Testament understand better than we do that real human events must take place in the group, in the context of human interaction, and that human interaction is never merely spiritual, sensory or private in nature. Therefore, it is not Jacob's special love for Joseph in and of itself that sparks this drama, but rather the display of this love. The gift of the robe was an event for witnesses to see, and having seen it, the brothers finally knew where they stood.

Verse 4b. "They hated him . . . " Much is said in these few opening lines of exposition. At this point, we are told that the open display of the father's favoritism has earned Joseph the hate of his brothers. Although this fact may seem easy enough for us to understand, we have to listen to this passage with great care. As was the case with the concept of favoritism, the concept of hate also requires a meticulous explanation. When we use the word "hate," we usually mean something that is a personal position or attitude. However, in the Hebrew, the verb "to hate" has a different meaning: it is a deed or the inception of a deed. To practice this kind of hate is like pulling a bowstring taut – it has no purpose unless an arrow is then unleashed. By the same token, hate makes no sense unless one follows through with a corresponding deed. Hate as a mere attitude would seem absurd to these people; to them it would be comparable to pulling the bowstring without an arrow. To them, hate as an attitude makes sense only as the definition of the time that separates the inception of this motion and the release of the bowstring. The tension resides within the person before the act, which then resolves it. For it is in the deed that hatred comes to fruition and is dissolved. This certainly has something to do with the fact that the people of that time were less likely to have repressed psychological complexes. Thus, when our storyteller says that the brothers hated Joseph, we should expect that a hate-fulfilling deed will follow.

Strangely enough, commentators on this passage rarely ask why the brothers did not simply direct their hatred toward their father. After all, what fault is it of Joseph that he had been set on a pedestal? Here, too, the storyteller displays his deep understanding of the human condition. He knows that because of the brothers' fear and respect for their elders, they dare not direct this kind of hatred at Jacob. Of course, their deed ends up wounding their father but, even so, they manage to maintain a facade of feigned innocence by remaining respectfully obedient to Jacob, and they bury their crime under a mountain of lies. In this, the storyteller has touched upon a bit of wisdom with which

he knows all of his hearers are familiar: the hatred of those
who have been slighted is targeted far more vehemently
against the favored one than it is against the one who does
the favoring, even when the favored one should not be
blamed. No example is really necessary to illustrate this
point, for nothing has really changed, and we modern
readers are just as aware of this truth as were the first hearers
of this story. Once again, we can recognize here a parallel
to the primeval story: Cain didn't direct his hatred toward
God, who favored Abel; instead, he hated the person who
was favored, Abel himself.

Verse 4c. "And [the brothers] could not speak peaceably
to him." The exact meaning of this fragment of the Hebrew
text is uncertain. Kittel and Procksch read here *dabber lo*,
which seems to indicate that the brothers were refusing to
greet Joseph. But even if this textual emendation is not
justified, the context does make it relatively plain that the
reference is to greetings. The breaking of fellowship between
Joseph and his brothers could in no way be more clearly
indicated. Even today, the withholding of a greeting is the
surest way to indicate the interruption of fellowship. In the
past, greetings were of an even greater significance in
community life, as the Old Testament demonstrates at many
different junctures. The well-being of the community,
"shalom," is maintained by the consistent use of greetings.
By asking about the health of others, and by saying
"welcome" and "goodbye," the individual is aware of his
or her belonging to the community, and shares this bond
with others. In this last phrase of v. 4, it is made amply clear
that the communal peace in the house of Jacob has been
broken.

37:5–11 *Joseph's dreams*

At this point, in the recounting of Joseph's two dreams, we
have the beginning of a second, separate explanation of the
conflict. The two explanations are set off from each other
by the rhetorical phrase, "they hated him even more," which
occurs at the end of v. 5 and is repeated at the end of v. 8.

The exhortation "Listen to this dream . . ." and the twice-
occuring *hinne* (a demonstrative particle that translates
loosely as "behold!") demonstrate the unmistakable
enthusiasm of the boy telling his dream. Joseph is

completely swept away by his dream, and he feels absolutely compelled to share it with his brothers. Otherwise it would be only potentially true that God reveals himself in dreams (see Genesis 28). Nothing is said of this here, and it seems quite clear that initially it is only Joseph who chooses to apply the dreams to himself. Even so, the possibility is left open that God is indeed revealing something in these dreams, something that will not be made clear until much later on. Thus, still at the very beginning of this story, we are confronted by a unique double layering of interpretations.

The narrating of the dreams is done with astonishing art, the hallmark of a narrative that was meant to be memorized and passed along verbally. The entire passage centers on verbs throughout, containing only two nouns. One of these nouns – the sheaves – occurs consistently throughout the account. The telling of the dream is by itself so clear that it requires no further explanations. The dream is a message for the brothers; it means to tell them something. And in v. 8, where we get the brothers' answer, it is equally plain that they do not hear any sort of divine revelation in this dream. All they hear is their brother talking and putting on airs, which infuriates them. They respond by demanding,

"Are you indeed to reign over us? Are you indeed to have dominion over us?"

Here it is worth noting that there is a parallelism of rhetorical parts in the brothers' counter-questions. We can observe how the speech framed in parallel form is distinguishable from the ordinary flux of the narration at those points where ordinary speech intensifies into a cry. Also interesting is the verb *malak*, meaning "to be a king" or "to reign." In this context, in a question directed to Joseph, the verb gains an ironic meaning, which corresponds with the use of the parallel verb *masal*, "to rule." After all, the brothers want neither Joseph nor anybody else as their king! To them, the very idea that anyone should rule over them seems horrible, to say nothing of the idea that this ruler should be their little brother. They are reacting not only to his willingness to lord it over them, but also to his pretension to rule over anyone at all. And in this, the brothers roughly outline for us what the dream means: in it, they hear the announcement of the will to future lordship and superiority. Referring once more to the text itself:

> "[Joseph's] sheaf rose and stood upright, then [the brothers'] sheaves gathered around it, and bowed down to [his] sheaf."

In these dreams, the fundamental preoccupation is with the question of authority over others. The fact that God is Lord has never been called into question in Israel; but up to this point, it had never been made very clear whether some human beings should be allowed to rule over others. The storyteller is writing in a time when the kingdom had taken firm root, but he is looking backwards to a time of patriarchs who knew no kingdoms – a time when the nomads abhorred the very idea of such a political state (see Joshua 9!). With this contrast in mind, the storyteller is asking: How is it possible and justifiable that in a nation one brother should lord it over the others? This is the question lurking behind Joseph's dreams.

Verses 9–11. The second dream is treated more briefly than the first. It is not so much the recounting of an event as it is a picture of a static moment. It represents the logical development of the first dream. The decisive predicate "to bow down" is used here just as it was before; the difference, however, is that Joseph now unabashedly names himself as the object of allegiance, and he now states that the circle of bowing figures includes his father and mother, as well. Thus, his father joins the angry reaction against the dream: "his father rebuked him." His father's reproachful question parallels the brothers' reaction to the first dream. Clearly, both brothers and father now stand against Joseph, which represents a change in the father's position since verses 3–4. Jacob asks, "What kind of dream is this that you have had"? The question is an expression of the shock he feels over a degenerate and abnormal dream through which God could not possibly have spoken, because it would be unprecedented and destructive of all order that a father and his sons should bow down before the youngest son. We need to understand this verb *histah^{a}wa* (to bow down) in its fullest weight of meaning for that time: whoever bows down before someone else thereby acknowledges that person as an absolute authority, and he puts himself completely at the disposal of that authority.

Verse 11b. Even though Jacob is shocked by Joseph's dream, and reproaches him, he remembers it. He heeds his son, for he is well aware of what dreams can mean. This becomes a mute testimony to the further development of the story. Joseph's dreams eventually come true, one by one. And already here we get a glimpse of the dual nature of these events, which will be revealed at the end (Genesis 50:20). The tension here comes from the consideration that, rather than being simply the product of Joseph's ambition, these dreams might actually be a hidden sign from God: "But his father kept the matter in mind."

37:12–17 *Transition: Jacob sends Joseph to his brothers*

The purpose of this transition is simply to set a new stage for Joseph. It is not possible to go into matters of geographical detail here, but suffice it to say that it is necessary that Joseph go to the place where his brothers are tending their animals. This is because what is about to transpire between him and his brothers must take place far away from their father. Joseph is supposed to check on the welfare of his brothers and of the flocks. Here we have again the orienting principle of *shalom*, which denotes wholeness, well-being, and a certain kind of inquiry as to how things are going. As events have now come to the verge of disaster, we are reminded once more what is at stake here: the issue is the well-being of the community as a whole, in which all living creatures – even the animals – are somehow involved. All things related to the life of the community are automatically linked to this well-being.

Joseph is not sure where he is going, and he wanders around the countryside, trying to find his way, until someone finally asks him what he is looking for. This small episode demonstrates just how lost and helpless Joseph is in the domain of his brothers. Out here, his father's preference is utterly useless – the paternal protection does not reach this far. Jacob's acts of favoritism have drawn a dangerous circle around the favored one: he becomes one thing inside the circle, and outside he becomes another. The very existence of the protective circle causes him to be doubly imperiled when he leaves it. This ought to cause us to reexamine our understanding of the very idea of protection, with its implications and consequences.

37:18–22   *The brothers' deadly attack*

Here we need to pause to clarify the biblical understanding of the idea of brotherhood. Our Christian usage of the term was formed in the New Testament. And yet we cannot really understand what "brother" means until we have examined its background in the Old Testament. This is because the New Testament's usage of the term is purely derivative. In its original and most fundamental usage, the word "brother" refers to someone who is first and foremost a member of a complete whole – the house or family. His membership is predicated on the fact that he is his parents' offspring, as is the membership of all the children. The siblings' common bond is their shared membership in the whole. On the one hand, this membership carries with it the right to a protected place at home and in the family. On the other hand, it also implies the obligation to stand up for the family if the need arises. Emotional attachments – such as brotherly love – are not necessarily a component of this concept of brotherhood and are certainly not constitutive of it. Solidarity of this kind is based on common membership in the family as a whole, and not on any kind of emotional ties to one another. Therefore, rivalry between maturing brothers is seen in the Old Testament as quite natural. Motives for conflict abound in these situations, and such conflicts are a central part of the story of the patriarchs. In fact, conflict between brothers is understood to be so normal and so forgivable that the conflict in and of itself usually does not even get in the way of a healthy relationship between siblings, as long as certain limits are obeyed and nothing is done that might harm the communal whole – the family. Unless we keep the original, Old Testament meaning of brotherhood in mind, we run the risk of succumbing to idealistic and sentimental misinterpretation of the relationships at hand. We must posit this sober and realistic understanding of brotherhood in what is now to follow.

Verse 18. "They saw him from a distance, and before he came near to them, they conspired to kill him." Here the story preserves an important point: this was the murderous design of a group of people, comparable to the premeditation of murder by an individual, and not merely a crime that springs from the heat of their anger. How are we to understand the brothers' ready willingness to agree on something like this? Every act of murder seeks to eliminate not only a human being, but also some sort of impediment in the murderer's path, and most murder motives tend to be based on jealousy or covetousness. Joseph stands between the brothers and their father's undivided love. His elevation to the status of favorite son has deprived them of something that is rightfully theirs. The motive for murder here is not very far removed from Cain's motive. Cain coveted God's loving attention just as the brothers of Joseph struggle for their father's favor. In both cases, a favorite son has become a barrier to someone else. And, also in both cases, the grievance is a just one. Cain, as well as Joseph's brothers, are unable to attack the injustice at its source, and herein lies the very root of their wicked acts. The crime is born out of mistrust.

Verses 18–20. The murder plot. Here, the plan to kill Joseph is linked directly to his dreams. Even though his brothers ridiculed him for his dreams, those dreams seem to have disturbed them. They know the possibility of premonitions of the future presenting themselves in dreams. In order to eliminate every possibility that this could happen, they will accept even the guilt of murdering their own brother.

37:21–22 *One brother intervenes*
Verse 21. Here the editor of the text most likely wrote "Reuben" in place of "Judah." Judah is the one who distances himself from the murder plot from the very outset. He resists the plan, saying, "Let us not take his life." And yet, he says "us," implying that even when refusing to take part in the action, he has not left their circle. Here we see a continuation of the peculiarly dichotomous origin of the deed: the brothers are concerned to protect their legitimate right, and in this even Judah participates.

Verse 22. Again the harshness of the plot is mitigated. Reuben does not openly oppose his brothers, as Judah does in v. 21. When Joseph appears, there is apparently a consensus on a single plan of action, and Reuben has kept secret his opposition to the murder, as well as his intent to save his brother.

What both of these accounts have in common is that the intervention comes from the eldest brother. There is a special significance to this, which also occurs elsewhere in the story of the patriarchs, but never as clearly as it does here. That significance lies in the issue of responsibility. In the extended households of old it happened often, as here, that parts of the family found themselves far away from their home and their father. During such periods, the father's role would pass temporarily to the eldest brother present. We can trace our understanding of the concept of responsibility back to these situations. Responsibility was a very real and concrete thing, for when the group returned to the father's house, the eldest brother would have to respond, quite literally, to the father's questions concerning all that had happened during the time of separation. All of his actions during the separation from his father are one in consciousness of this answer he will have to give his father. The authority that is bestowed on the eldest brother during these times is not his own; it is merely transferred authority, which he must return to his father as soon as the group returns and he must give account before his father. Only the father has real and original authority. The eldest's responsibility is not based on some kind of feeling of responsibility or even a sense of duty, but rather out of a simple realization that it is he who must give account. It rapidly becomes clear that the story of Joseph is very much concerned with the many different roles involved in being a brother – that of the youngest, the eldest, and the others.

37:23–30 *The deed*

Verse 23. On Joseph's arrival, the very first thing that the brothers do is rip from his body the robe, the symbol of the favoritism which has provoked their wrath. At this point, there is a sudden break in the action, the brothers sit down to eat a meal. This pause separates their first act against Joseph from the following, and creates the possibility that there could still be a new beginning. Our attention is called to the stylized portrayal of Joseph at this point. So far, he has not said a word (except his request for directions along the way), and he has taken no action. Now he continues his silence, neither complaining nor asking what is going on, passively allowing events to overtake him. This is certainly a deliberate portrayal, which contrasts the Joseph of the beginning of the story with the Joseph of the end more strongly and clearly than could our modern narrative technique, which at this point would seize the opportunity to portray the effect on Joseph of his brothers' actions.

Verse 25b. And then, in a rather simple turn of events, we have the arrival of a *deus ex machina* in the form of the Ishmaelite caravan. With their appearance, the story gains a realistic, historical background. The caravan is making its way from Gilead to Egypt, and it is known that the route for caravans actually passed Dothan. The trade between east Jordan and Egypt presupposed in this passage existed at that time, and passed exactly on this route.

Verse 26. Judah's suggestion connects with the situation as it was in v. 21. He warns his brothers of the consequences of their plot. According to one narrator, both the deed and its consequences are apparent to all the brothers from the very beginning. In the other account, however, the brothers start out only with the deed itself in mind, and the intervening brother has to point out the consequences to them.

Judah reminds them of the consequences with the phrase, "If we kill our brother and conceal his blood . . ." If we put ourselves in their situation, we can't help but feel the effect of Judah's choice of words – "our brother," he says. And the effect is heightened by the fact that, with the second verb, he includes the deed's consequences as part of the deed itself. Judah is taking his responsibilities as the eldest son seriously in that his words show him to have thought ahead of his brothers in order to remind them what the moment of action will truly entail. They will have to conceal their brother's blood. Can they do such a thing? The parallels in Genesis 4:10 and Job 16:18 serve as warnings – even concealed blood is capable of crying out!

Verse 27. Judah shows them another way. His suggestion is included in the warning against the alternative course of action. Here again, we see a surprising psychological subtlety at work: Judah assents to his brothers' desire, but disagrees with their method. His concern is not only with keeping himself out of a dirty business – he tries to win his brothers over to his way of thinking.

Verse 27b. "And his brothers agreed." This short, very pregnant sentence is the turning point of this entire narrative. The crux of this moment is the fact that the brothers heed Judah, and in so doing, assent to his alternative plan. The storyteller's great skill appears in the fact that no motives are actually explained, either for Judah's initial intervention or for the brothers' eventual consent. At this critical juncture in the story, the things that are unspoken speak for themselves.

Verse 28. The decisive moment has already taken place. All that is necessary now is a short account of the execution of the deed. The agreed-upon plot has already been sealed, and the payment in cash serves as the proof. They have in hand the "average price for a half-grown boy, Leviticus 27:4f" (Gunkel). Normally, the fact that Joseph has been sold into slavery by his brothers would be a grave crime. But here, in the context of the story which it concludes, it seems less a crime and more an act of salvation.

37:24, 28a, c., 29, 30   The deed

On the surface, the brothers' first deed seems to be a collective action. In reality, however, they allow their plan for a bloodless murder to become reality while Reuben, by the same action, does his best to set in motion his own secret plan to save Joseph. Both of these intentions are contained in the last sentence of v. 24: "The pit was empty; there was no water in it."

According to the one storyteller, the traders are Midianites (compare with Judges 8:22 and 24). At any rate, both storytellers have the same people in mind. These traveling merchants have very different functions in the accounts of the two storytellers. On the one hand, they represent a turning point at the moment of highest tension. On the other hand, the Midianites are the source of a new twist in the plot – an added complication. Here (v. 28c), where the story reads, "And they took Joseph to Egypt," we have the interference of an outside force, which gets in the way of the brothers' murder plot as well as Reuben's planned rescue. Thus, the caravan's departure has different results in the two versions of the story. In the first, the traders leave behind a circle of brothers which is once again united. In the other, they leave behind a divided circle of brothers who have all been equally surprised by the latest turn of events. The defining phrase of the first version is: "His brothers agreed"; in the second version, events are defined by the sudden intrusion of foreign merchants. At this point, the two versions diverge significantly.

Verse 29. Here is the dramatic high point of this story – not the deed itself, but the deed's consequences as they are felt by the one brother. At this high point, the brothers have been divided. And here we have yet another disconcerting point – Reuben's dismay at finding the pit empty is so great that it actually overshadows the father's subsequent grief.

Verse 30. Reuben returns to his brothers. Now he finally opens himself up to them by bitterly complaining to them about Joseph's disappearance. We would expect some kind of reaction from the brothers, but nothing more is heard from them.

37:31–36   In the father's house, the concealment of the deed
Verse 31. One of the storytellers explains the reason for the robe with astonishing clarity: it is the gift representing a father's favoritism; a symbol of superiority; the object of a hatred that grows into action; the falsified evidence. As such, it is the cause of Jacob's heart-rending complaint, and it consolidates the guilt of the brothers, who show themselves capable of mutely standing by as their father suffers. All that is left of a father's special love is a mournful sorrow that will not be assuaged. The brothers are helpless in this new situation; they try, unsuccessfully, to rouse their father out of his sadness. He refuses all comfort (compare Genesis 38:12 and Jeremiah 31:15). By remaining in a state of mourning, he is attempting to maintain contact with his son. He no longer has any use for peace or wholeness. And thus, the brothers have achieved nothing by their half-executed deed. They have not regained what they were after.

Application

A sermon on Genesis 37 would either have to concentrate solely on the plot line or else concentrate on a full examination of a single portion of the text. Even a Bible study group should have at least two or three hours to understand this chapter better. The point of departure for the presentation can follow from the explanation given here. The question of the significance of the family in our day and age can be approached by considering another question: What does the Bible mean when it speaks of the brother?

Here we will have to begin with our Christian use of language in forms of address such as "brothers and sisters" and in the affirmation, "we are all brothers!" We need to be aware of the ever-present danger that such generalized reference to the "brother" or "sister" can easily become empty, thoughtless, or sentimental.

This story urges us to reflect on what a brother really is, and how the Bible treats brotherhood. If we do this, many of our illusions will fall by the wayside, the principle of which is that there is such a thing as a generic, generalized "brother." The more we refer to such an abstraction, the less we understand the term and the less we really say about it. Thus the story of the Bible leads us into a story which tells about what really happened among real brothers.

Among these particular brothers, the overriding issue is peace, by which is meant the soundness of the community. We must try to understand this definition of peace with the same kind of fresh objectivity with which we approach the idea of brother, we must see it as something new, devoid of sentimentality.

After having been led to the text in this way, we have nothing more to do than to lead our hearers into the events which it contains. To bring to life the individual sections and scenes of the narrative, to show them the high points and turning points, and now and again to move from the individual events to call attention to the great movements and theological concepts that lie behind the individual events.

The purpose of the presentation of this chapter of the story of Joseph is not to provide us with either universal truths or handy applications of the same. The purpose is rather to allow that which happened here to speak for itself and to allow a portion of biblical events to take on life for their hearers by simply permitting them to speak in their own narrative power.

2

Joseph's Fall and Rise (Genesis 39:1–23)

Text

39 Now Joseph was taken down to Egypt, and Potiphar, an officer of
Pharaoh, the captain of the guard, an Egyptian, bought him from
the Ishmaelites who had brought him down there. ²The LORD was
with Joseph, and he became a successful man; he was in the house
of his Egyptian master. ³His master saw that the LORD was with
him, and that the LORD caused all that he did to prosper in his
hands. ⁴So Joseph found favor in his sight and attended him; he
made him overseer of his house and put him in charge of all that he
had. ⁵From the time that he made him overseer in his house and
over all that he had, the LORD blessed the Egyptian's house for
Joseph's sake; the blessing of the LORD was on all that he had, in
house and field. ⁶So he left all that he had in Joseph's charge; and,
with him there, he had no concern for anything but the food that he
ate.

Now Joseph was handsome and good-looking. ⁷And after a time his
master's wife cast her eyes on Joseph and said, "Lie with me." ⁸But
he refused and said to his master's wife, "Look, with me here, my
master has no concern about anything in the house, and he has put
everything that he has in my hand. ⁹He is not greater in this house
than I am, nor has he kept back anything from me except yourself,
because you are his wife. How then could I do this great wickedness,
and sin against God?" ¹⁰And although she spoke to Joseph day after
day, he would not consent to lie beside her or to be with her. ¹¹One
day, however, when he went into the house to do his work, and
while no one else was in the house, ¹²she caught hold of his garment,
saying, "Lie with me!" But he left his garment in her hand, and
fled and ran outside. ¹³When she saw that he had left his garment
in her hand and had fled outside, ¹⁴she called out to the members of
her household and said to them, "See, my husband has brought
among us a Hebrew to insult us! He came in to me to lie with me,
and I cried out with a loud voice; ¹⁵and when he heard me raise my
voice and cry out, he left his garment beside me, and fled outside."

21

¹⁶*Then she kept his garment by her until his master came home,*
¹⁷*and she told him the same story, saying, "The Hebrew servant,*
whom you have brought among us, came in to me to insult me;
¹⁸*but as soon as I raised my voice and cried out, he left his garment*
beside me, and fled outside."

19 When his master heard the words that his wife spoke to him
saying, "This is the way your servant treated me," he became
enraged. ²⁰And Joseph's master took him and put him into the prison,
the place where the king's prisoners were confined; he remained
there in prison. ²¹But the LORD was with Joseph and showed him
steadfast love; he gave him favor in the sight of the chief jailer.

²²The chief jailer committed to Joseph's care all the prisoners who
were in the prison, and whatever was done there, he was the one
who did it. ²³The chief jailer paid no heed to anything that was in
Joseph's care, because the LORD was with him; and whatever he did,
the LORD made it prosper.

Structure

The story in chapter 39 is constructed in the following
manner:

1–6	Joseph among the Egyptians
7–20	Joseph's innocent downfall
21–23	Joseph's exaltation while in prison

Interpretation

In verses 1–3 Joseph becomes the slave of an Egyptian. The
Egyptian is not given a name until a later stage of the
narrative, a very frequent characteristic of this kind of
narrative which we also encounter, for example, in the
Synoptic Gospels.

The unifying motif in chapter 39 is that God was with
Joseph. The presence of God is an essential part of blessing.
This is a concept which can be traced far back into the history
of religions and which appears, for example, in Sumerian
mythology in the following manner: one who would
undertake a journey into the territory ruled by a certain

god must first make sure whether this god will be for him
or against him. Something similar is meant here. God was
on Joseph's side, which meant promotion and benefit for
him. Yahweh gave him success, as the second sentence says.
In the history of the patriarchs, God's blessing (defined in
part by God's presence) is one of the principal theological
concepts. Here we can observe how the story of Joseph
carries on the ancient motifs of the history of the patriarchs,
as we see, for instance, in the story of Jacob living in the
house of Laban. God's blessing and presence is never
explained; either it is there or it is not. When Yahweh here
blesses Joseph in a foreign land – which also implies that
he is living in the territory of other gods – this need not
lead us to speak of "Universalism," as does, for instance,
Procksch. Rather, what we have at work here is the ancient
understanding that the "God of the Fathers" belongs not to
any particular land, but to a group of nomadic people (A.
Alt). The Egyptian perceives this presence of God with
Joseph, that is to say, he sees that Joseph has success, and
that impresses him. Here we can clearly observe how that
which we today call success or happiness was at one time
considered to be obviously anchored in the acts of God,
and to be the result of God's activity. But when this blessing
happens in a foreign land, it is the visible side of this
blessing, that is, the success which everyone can see, which
appears to be most important.

Verses 4–5. "So Joseph found favor in his sight." We need
to hear these words very literally, for they reflect the
communal life. The new turn in events is manifested in the
fact that Joseph is seen by his master in a new way, that as
he stands before him to receive his orders he finds a new
affection and favor in his eyes. In the world of this story,
important processes and changes are not to be read from
the interior life of a person, as, for instance, in these
ponderings of Joseph's master, but rather in the open
displays that come about in the common face-to-face
dealings between one person and his fellows. (Compare this
with the above observations about the partiality and
preference which Joseph enjoyed.) We can see this clearly
in the following manner. There would be no difficulty
in having v. 4b follow directly after v. 3: "His master saw
that . . . and he made him overseer in his house and put

him in charge of all that he had." For us, there would seem
to be nothing missing at this point. For the narrator,
however, the most important thing would be missing,
because for him, the real new development consists of the
fact that the master has now come to see his servant in a
new light, and that the servant has found something new
in his eyes, namely, favor.

"And he made him overseer in his house." On this,
Gunkel remarks that such major-domos can often be seen
in Egyptian pictures, usually with a staff or a role of paper
in their hands. Yahweh is on Joseph's side, showering him
with success, and this comes to have a wider effect on the
house of the Egyptian as soon as Joseph has been appointed
overseer. For blessing has a growing and pervasive power,
just as it does in the story of Jacob in Laban's house.

39:6b, 7–20   *Joseph's innocent downfall*

The fact that Joseph was handsome in stature and
appearance is mentioned here not in the interest of having
a precise description, but because it promotes our
understanding of the episode which it introduces. Joseph's
good looks are important neither in themselves nor because
of any help they might give us in forming a mental image
of him, but only because of the possibilities inherent in his
handsomeness. In the Old Testament, beauty always is more
of a process than a static quality. Human beauty is always
seen primarily as something which becomes significant in
relationships between people, as, for example, in the Song
of Songs.

Verse 7. The sentence: "And his master's wife cast her
eyes on Joseph" corresponds to our concept of desire. While
we lay the emphasis on the internal phenomenon within
the soul of the individual, in this narrative it falls on that
which happens between two persons.

"And [she] said, 'lie with me'" In v. 10 an editor tones
that down to: "to be with her." At a later period the
expression had come to sound offensively crass. There had
been a loss of appreciation for how well a direct manner of
speech can convey the directness of human sexual
relationships. When no one dares any longer to give sexual
realities an unequivocal name, it is evidence that attitudes
toward them have become faulty and broken. When our

story is read dispassionately, it is undeniable that this happening is described with real shame, on the one hand, and with great naturalness, on the other. In those places where shame seeks to hide too much, the story loses its genuineness and becomes questionable.

Verse 8. "But he refused, and said . . ." On this Gunkel remarks: "The narrator contrasts the lasciviousness of the Egyptian woman with the chastity of the Israelite youth." And Procksch entitles it "the motif of the pure man confronting the impure woman," and then remarks, "Through the projection (of the Egyptian intention) on to Joseph, the contrast between the modest Semite and the wicked Hamite is artfully brought into play." Both of these commentators have totally missed the meaning of the story. According to them, the contrast which governs the narrative is that of the two characteristics (chastity and licentiousness; purity and impurity) personified by the principal characters. But such a juxtaposition of attributes misunderstands the story, and at its decisive point. This failure to understand can be explained in terms of the profound involvement in abstract and moralistic thinking in which we live, a kind of thought which is totally alien to this narrative. If this kind of contrast were really the point, what could we make of the remark that Joseph's acquiesence would have meant a breach of trust? If the purpose had really been to highlight the contrast between chastity and lasciviousness, that could have been done much more effectively if no other motives had contributed toward the decision.

In another of his comments, Gunkel refers to the real scope (*Skopos*) of the narrative: "Joseph rejects her demand because it would be a serious breach of confidence, and this is a feature which recurs in every version of the story." Thus Joseph refuses to betray the trust which his master has deposited in him. All of the talk about the "chaste Joseph," then, misses the real meaning of the story, as do all of the numerous graphic portrayals of this scene which are predicated on this error. What Joseph says to his master's wife in reply to her proposition is based on this argument: ". . . nor has he kept back anything from me except yourself, because you are his wife." These introductory sentences demonstrate how comprehensive Joseph's authority is. The entire oversight of the house is in his hands, and he has been granted wide discretionary powers. At this one point, however, his power is expressly limited. Because of the woman's demand, he is given the opportunity to break even that one restriction. Then the dominion of his master would have become nothing but an illusion. Joseph just says no. He honors the imposed delimitation because he sees behind it the kindness of his lord, the favor which he had found in his eyes. It is this *kindness* which establishes the limit for him. "How then could I do this great wickedness . . .?" He knows that his acceptance of the woman's demand would be a betrayal of his lord's gracious favor.

The conventional commentary on this episode, which we have rejected in the discussion above, separates the instant of temptation out of the totality of what happened, and creates the fiction that the focus of the events consisted simply in the encounter of man and woman in the instant of temptation, as if all were to be decided in a struggle between the powers of sexual attraction and the opposing power of chastity or purity. The decisive issue in our story is rather to be found in the fact that the woman's demand is confronted by an entirely different power, Joseph's loyalty to his master, who had given him his trust.

In the blurring and dislocation of this central message of the Joseph story by modern interpreters is revealed the perverse view of sexual acts in general, which are isolated and singled out in a special way as the objects of moral judgments. The false understanding of the Joseph story is a classic example thereof. This false and ostensibly modest singling out of sexual realities reveals itself, for instance, in the strange expression, "sex life." One has become accustomed to think and act as if this were a separate area of human life which needed to be maintained as isolated as possible, and in which all thought and action about sexual matters depended on an isolated decision between chastity and the libido, between purity and impurity. The Joseph story can show us how fundamentally wrong this attitude is. For one cannot simply isolate thought and action of this kind to one area of life. In any case, decisions made in this area will extend themselves into the totality of existence and therefore into all of life. They can never be limited to an illusory "sexual" area of life. In our narrative, Joseph's acceptance of the woman's demand would have been, before everything else, a decision against his master and a breach of his trust. Propriety in sexual matters depends on the strength of non-sexual relationships.

Verse 9. "How then could I do this great wickedness, and sin against God?" Now it is clear, the sin in question here is not sexual impurity but the breach of the trust which Joseph's lord had deposited in him. The limit which is given Joseph in his administration is one which is watched over by God. God guards this boundary. Inside of it God protects and preserves the integrity and peace of society. This is also done in Egypt. That the breach of this trust brings with it also an offense against God is understood even by this Egyptian woman, who serves other gods. Joseph experienced God's presence in his own progress and exaltation. He experiences divine governance in the boundary which is drawn for him, in the limit constructed out of the experience of his good fortune. The boundary of God's governance clearly arises here out of divine presence and gifts. It is a beautiful and clear example of how God's commandments are related to God's goodness. The breach of trust would be a sin against God because that trust was a gift from God.

Verses 11–18. The dramatic progression toward a crisis is portrayed in an uncomplicated manner. Verses 7–9 tell of events which occur only once, while v. 10 adds the continual repetition which must lead to a crisis, and in vv. 11–18 the story is told again as a one-time occurrence. Joseph's refusal is put to increasingly severe tests. And because it is the wife of his master who demands the "great wickedness" from him, he cannot avoid this testing, but must endure it. Once more we note the effectiveness of simple artistic methods, for in this portrayal of increasing tension leading to crisis there is no psychological fleshing-out of details. This narrative style serves well to underscore the progression toward the inevitable crisis.

In v. 11 the stage is set. Joseph enters the house as a part of his daily round of work, and finds himself alone. This introduction to the event in progress is masterful in its economy of expression. The description of the action in vv. 12ff is discreet and sober. Simply the laconic brevity of the report eliminates any possibility of undue attention to detail. This severe sobriety of expression, which calls things by their names without filling in details, is not of the kind which would promote any kind of curious excitement.

The fact that Joseph is obliged to flee from a woman, a sad and shameful thing for him, is another result of his situation, for she is the wife of his master. The result of his flight on the woman, the transformation of her love into hate, is portrayed artfully in v. 13, a partial repetition of v. 12: " When she saw that . . ." Once more here, as in v. 3 and v. 7, the act of seeing has an accentuated meaning. One can, in fact, understand the entire episode from the perspective of the three kinds of seeing that occur: the Egyptian looks at Joseph (v. 3); his wife looks at Joseph (v. 7); the woman sees the garment left behind. Commenting on the story for ourselves, we say that the woman's love is transformed into hatred. But that is perhaps a too hasty conclusion, for that which happens here can probably not really be expressed in emotionally loaded concepts of this kind.

Once more, though in an entirely different manner than in chapter 37, it is a garment which brings public attention to what had been a very private event. The silence of a hidden event is broken by a scream. In this way the lady of the house calls the servants to be her witnesses. Although they have seen nothing, the woman knows how she will nevertheless turn them into witnesses. She begins very cleverly by declaring herself to be on the side of the servants: "See, my husband has brought among us a Hebrew to insult us!" When she says "he" she is speaking of the lord, as do the domestic servants. Though she is taking sides with them against Joseph, there is also a suggestion of criticism of her husband. Suddenly, Joseph has become "a Hebrew." Gunkel's comment is apt, "She dabbles a bit in anti-Semitism." All of this constitutes a masterful description, especially when we note that when the woman reports her version of what has happened, she uses almost precisely the same words with which the real event had previously been objectively described (compare vv. 12b; 15b; 18b). Here we note once more the astonishing attention to the human element on the part of one of the narrators. He knows – and applies masterfully in his narrative – that if one wants to conceal a certain fact, the wisest course is to stick as close as possible to reality, hoping that in this way the departures from the truth will be almost imperceptible. Once more the garment becomes circumstantial evidence, it is ripped away from Joseph by the woman who loves and desires him and with this act hurls him into the depths. Though the economical style of narration does not make the ascription of motivation necessary, the hearers may do so on their own if they wish.

Verses 16–18. The wife tells her husband the same story. The transition is v. 16, which is like a momentary still image among the hastening action. The woman remains lying down, the evidence at her side. Her husband, too, is not only to hear, but also to visualize. He, too, gets a share of the blame as she tells him (v. 17): "The Hebrew servant, whom you have brought among us . . ." Here we have another subtlety, for this particular part of her false accusation is entirely true! She would not need to alter this statement in the least if she were to tell the truth. It is the old story of pushing the guilt onto others, as also in Genesis 3: "The woman whom you gave to be with me . . ."

Verses 19–20. The man listens to his wife, and his anger flares up. He does not listen to Joseph. After hearing this statement from his wife, who had probably also prudently enlisted the servants as witnesses, there is no chance at all of saving Joseph. Only now does Joseph grasp how hard his fate is to be. He is a slave. When, at a later time in their history, the people of Israel were constantly being told, "Remember that you were a slave in Egypt," and thus exhorted to be kind and just to slaves, one of their strongest motivations must have been their horror at the defenselessness of this man who, through no fault of his own, had come to be a slave of a people of many great lords. But the narrator does not exploit this theme with even a line of reflection, and the hearer must sense it from the story.

More important, however, is the theological aspect of the narration. What kind of a God is this, who simply permits that Joseph sink into the depths, a man who has refused to commit a great sin against him? And what about God's presence with Joseph? These questions remain unanswered, and that he is permitted to fall is not justified or explained with a single word. So single-minded is the narrator in his purpose to tell the works of God. It is just not possible to ask God to explain his actions afterward. Joseph is not counting on God. He does not despair, nor does he even

pose a question. And there is no word about the punishment
of the guilty woman. All of that can simply remain open
and unfinished business. It is sufficient that God's action
continues.

It is necessary to say a word about the literary heritage
of vv. 7–20. As commentators remark, this episode is based
on a widely-known motif. It appears in an Egyptian story
about two brothers. But Gunkel is of the opinion that there
are Indian and Persian versions which have more in
common with this story than does the Egyptian. It is thereby
established, however, that we are dealing here not with
literary dependence, but rather with a link to the pre-history
of the story, which has to be understood in relation to its
pre-literary stage. It is probable that the narrator has here
selected a narrative motif which is familiar to him and
adapted it for the purposes of his story. The special message
here lies in the manner in which he has adapted the subtlest
nuances of the old motif to fit this particular story.

39:21–23 *Joseph's exaltation while in prison*
When one compares these verses with 39:2f., one encounters
a number of identical or almost identical statements, so that
it would almost be possible to speak of variations. Now,
God is once more with Joseph. He shows him grace (*haesed*),
which is not presented as an attribute of God but as a
description of God's activity. This grace takes form in the
fact that Joseph again finds favor with his new superior,
who is this time the overseer of the prison. Just as the
Egyptian had done previously, so the warden entrusts
everything to him. And once more, God gives him success
in everything he does.

The narrator's attitude about God's action is made amply
clear here. That God is with a certain person does not signify
that everything will therefore always go well, or that he or
she will always be spared ruin and humiliation. God is free,
totally free in his actions toward human beings, and God's
acts toward human kind are by no means always simply
reactive responses to human attitudes and actions toward
God. If God were not free and unpredictable in these
matters, God would not be God. One thing, however, can
be counted on: wherever an individual or a society has been
involved in God's story, this story will continue, even

though during long periods they may sense nothing of it. The narrator sees God's action toward humankind with just as much realism as he sees the communality and conflicts among human beings. Though the manner of God's activity cannot be quantified in formulas, it is enough to know that God takes a hand in human history.

Application

In the presentation of this chapter it will be necessary to remember that we are accustomed by the churchly language of worship, Bible study and catechetics to speak of God and humankind in general and comprehensive terms. We speak about sin and grace and justification, about the Law and the Gospel. We say that "the human being" is a sinner, that the forgiveness of sins has happened for everyone, and things of this kind.

On the other hand, at our Church gatherings (*Kirchentagen*), adult education seminars and retreats, we talk only about "topics of current interest," about modern music and modern warfare, about population limitation and foreign aid, and so on. Unfortunately we have to admit that we continue to find it as difficult as always to discover natural transitions from our generalized theological statements about God and humanity to these contemporary issues. In spite of our efforts, for many simple Christians these things continue to be separate worlds which cannot be brought together.

It is with this difficulty in mind that we should hear this section of the story of Joseph. The first thing we will then discover is that the Bible story that we are hearing is one in which people are described as they really are. And the events described here are a portrayal of life as it really is. Here we find no generalizations, no slogans, no concepts which reduce everything to sameness. That which happens here is unmistakeably unique (*einmalig*) and authentic.

And into these genuine happenings from life which are presented with interest and color, God enters with divine action. It is not always easy to recognize, and the attempt to sum it up in generalized statements can destroy it. Rather than that, all depends on our willingness to throw ourselves profoundly into these events, to move through them step by step, and to take very seriously the human element in the story.

We will not try to fit the temptation described here into any generalized scheme of temptations, but try instead to think it through in its ordinariness and uniqueness, and then perhaps take a look at the possible temptations to which we ourselves are subject, and in which something special always crosses a person's path, something in which that person participates in all of his or her humanity, and which becomes a special event in that person's own story with God.

Finally, when we have walked through this narrative in all its phases and with all of that which it does not say, but only intimates, we can move from this story to think about the Incarnation, about God's assumption of human flesh. This human condition into which God descends is nothing generalized, abstract, and contrived, but the real individual human existence with all its highs and lows. It is for this reason that the Bible is so intensely interested in that which is purely human, as our story shows.

3

Preparation for Joseph's Exaltation
(Genesis 40:1–23)

Text

40 *Some time after this, the cupbearer of the king of Egypt and his baker offended their lord the king of Egypt. ²Pharaoh was angry with his two officers, the chief cupbearer and the chief baker, ³and he put them in custody in the house of the captain of the guard, in the prison where Joseph was confined. ⁴The captain of the guard charged Joseph with them, and he waited on them; and they continued for some time in custody. ⁵One night they both dreamed – the cupbearer and the baker of the king of Egypt, who were confined in the prison – each his own dream, and each dream with its own meaning. ⁶When Joseph came to them in the morning, he saw that they were troubled. ⁷So he asked Pharaoh's officers, who were with him in custody in his master's house, "Why are your faces downcast today?" ⁸They said to him, "We have had dreams, and there is no one to interpret them." And Joseph said to them, "Do not interpretations belong to God? Please tell them to me."*

9 *So the chief cupbearer told his dream to Joseph, and said to him, "In my dream there was a vine before me, ¹⁰and on the vine there were three branches. As soon as it budded, its blossoms came out and the clusters ripened into grapes. ¹¹Pharaoh's cup was in my hand; and I took the grapes and pressed them into Pharaoh's cup, and placed the cup in Pharaoh's hand." ¹²Then Joseph said to him, "This is its interpretation: the three branches are three days; ¹³within three days Pharaoh will lift up your head and restore you to your office; and you shall place Pharaoh's cup in his hand, just as you used to do when you were his cupbearer. ¹⁴But remember me when it is well with you; please do me the kindness to make mention of me to Pharaoh, and so get me out of this place. ¹⁵For in fact I was stolen out of the land of the Hebrews; and here also I have done nothing that they should have put me into the dungeon."*

16 *When the chief baker saw that the interpretation was favorable, he said to Joseph, "I also had a dream: there were three cake baskets*

on my head, [17]*and in the uppermost basket there were all sorts of baked food for Pharaoh, but the birds were eating it out of the basket on my head." [18]And Joseph answered. "This is its interpretation: the three baskets are three days; [19]within three days Pharaoh will lift up your head – from you! – and hang you on a pole; and the birds will eat the flesh from you."*

20 *On the third day, which was Pharaoh's birthday, he made a feast for all his servants, and lifted up the head of the chief cupbearer and the head of the chief baker among his servants.* [21]*He restored the chief cupbearer to his cupbearing, and he placed the cup in Pharaoh's hand;* [22]*but the chief baker he hanged, just as Joseph had interpreted to them.* [23]*Yet the chief cupbearer did not remember Joseph, but forgot him.*

Structure

The narrative in chapter 40 is structured in this way:

(There are connections back to chapters 37 and 36 and fragments in 39:1, 2, 4, 6.)

1–4   Introduction: two of Pharaoh's officials are brought into the prison, and Joseph is to be their servant

5–19   The dreams and their interpretation

    5–8   The dreams of the officials and Joseph's inquiry

    9–13   The chief butler's dream and Joseph's interpretation

    14–15   Joseph's request

    16–19   The chief baker's dream and Joseph's interpretation

20–22   The fulfillment of the interpretation

23   The forgotten request

Interpretation

Seen in the context of the whole story, this chapter is an

expansion that grows out of the special interest in dreams that can be traced through the entire story. Nothing really happens to Joseph himself in the entire chapter, which ends with the statement that he has been forgotten and will have to remain in prison. This is consciously retarding in its effect, and summarily severs the expectation, which had been growing in the chapter, that Joseph's lot would now certainly have to begin to improve.

1. Dreams

Dreams are so important for the narrator that he inserts here, by means of his own conspicuous scene, a dream interpretation which is to prepare the way for the definitive interpretation of dreams which will come in chapter 41. What is significant about these dreams and their interpretation? In the story of the patriarchs there are frequent reports which tell how God revealed himself to one of the patriarchs and gave him a word of instruction or promise. That is different in the story of Joseph, which contains no accounts of God's immediate self-revelation to human beings. This has to do with the Joseph story's origin in a later epoch with a more "enlightened" spirituality. Because of the prevalence of that kind of intellectual atmosphere, a form of revelation in which a natural phenomenon like a dream is the vehicle of revelation assumes special importance. We can assume that behind this narrative motif stands a great and meaningful complex of traditions; the actual transmission of God's word and will through the dream, which at one time must have had important meaning and wide dissemination. We learn about it much later in the polemics of the prophets against others, the so-called prophets of salvation, in Jeremiah 23:25 and 28:

> "I have heard what the prophets have said who prophesy lies in my name, saying 'I have dreamed, I have dreamed!'"

> "Let the prophet who has a dream tell the dream, but let the one who has my word speak my word faithfully."

When Jeremiah here speaks out against a degenerate prophetism in which the prophet appeals to a dream, it is to be assumed that behind it lies a long tradition in which such revelation through dreams once had an entirely positive meaning. We can assume that that which is said here in the Joseph narrative about divine revelation through dreams belongs to the very beginning of this line of tradition. An essential difference lies in the fact that here the dream had not yet been ascribed to prophetism, so that neither the dreams nor their interpretation had been linked to any office. But now it is precisely our narrative which reveals a decisive point of departure, alluded to in v. 8: "Do not interpretations belong to God?" When we compare the dreams of chapter 37 (there, as here, a co-ordinated pair!), we note that nothing is said there about interpretation. Nor is it necessary, since those dreams speak directly for themselves. That is probably determined through the simplicity of the societal form in which the dream occurs. In the very complex conditions in Egypt, on the other hand, it can happen that a person receives a message from God in a dream, but is incapable of interpreting it. That the interpretation belongs to God implies that God himself must give someone the ability to interpret the dream, and call him to do so. Here we can see very clearly the transition from the immediacy of a divine revelation in a dream to a revelation that is no longer direct, but mediated through a mediator gifted and called for that purpose. The third stage is then that in which the dream itself can no longer be that of just any person, for only the dreams of special mediators as, for example, the prophets, can transmit divine revelations.

These differing stages of meaning of the dream as the vehicle of a divine revelation can be sketched here only in broad outlines. For the purpose of our story, it is important only to understand that behind the narrative motif stands genuine history, the real meaning of the dreams for the transmission of words of God in an early time in Israel's history. When it is told here how helpless and unhappy the Egyptian officials are at their inability to interpret the two dreams they have had (we shall see how in the next chapter just this motif is heightened), and when we see, on the other hand, that it is the alien slave who knows that he is empowered by God to interpret the dreams, we are able to perceive directly the thankful joy over this gift which God has given to those whom he has chosen and with whom he abides. In this narrative we have a reflection of Israel's actual experience during its early history of interpreting God's will and word through dreams.

We need to pay special attention to the occasion which led to the interpretation of the dreams of the two Egyptian officials in prison. Joseph, as we are told, had been given to them as a servant in the prison. We are told with great vivacity how Joseph comes into their cell in the morning:

> When Joseph came to them in the morning, he saw that they were troubled. So he asked Pharaoh's officers . . . Why are your faces downcast today?

In order to understand this stage of the story, one must understand the atmosphere of a prison. Only then can one judge the meaning of such an interested question. The entire event which follows here provokes human solidarity. This simple interest in others is assigned great importance by our narrative. It is an example of the human interest which is so characteristic of the entire story of Joseph. It is, moreover, important to note that this sympathy with human beings does not depend on extraordinary events or statements, but remains within the bounds of that simple inquiry into the welfare of others which is common to all people. Here our story gives silent witness to what a great significance these simple, common forms of human encounter can have when they are not mere dry formalities but lively expressions of real interest in other people. We are reminded of the statement in 37:4, where it is said of the brothers that after their father's gift to Joseph "they could not speak peaceably to him." In these early biblical narratives, the ordinary forms of human conversation are credited with decisive importance for human relations. That Joseph looked at the two prisoners, noticed the sadness in their demeanor, and then asked them the reason – all of this serves the narrator's purpose of showing that Joseph treated the two prisoners as fellow human beings.

Although the two dreams of the chief butler and the chief baker are clear enough in their meaning, it is nevertheless necessary to note the subtle difference between the dreams and Joseph's interpretation of them. For it is evident that

the decisive difference between the two dreams is entirely
passed over in the interpretation. This contrast consists in
the fact that one dream describes a positive event, the other
a troubled one. This contrast is the basis of the interpretation
that one man will be restored to his responsibilities and the
other executed. What is expressed in Joseph's interpretation
are only features of secondary importance, as, for example,
that the three branches mean three days. It would be
possible to speak of an allegorical interpretation of the
secondary features, and it is possible that the allegorical
interpretation itself has its origin in the interpretation. In
that which is decisive, however, the dreams are not
interpreted by allegory but by direct correspondence
between the action of the dream and real events. The
interpretation of the dreams of the Egyptians narrated here
presupposes already-existent interpretive skill; in the
interpretation of dreams we encounter the actual beginnings
of hermeneutics.

Because, in our day, dreams are being taken more
seriously as an expression of the human condition than they
have been for centuries, and because a scholarly
interpretation of dreams now exists (stemming from
medicine and psychology; compare the various schools of
psychoanalysis, such as that of Jung, which concern
themselves with dreams), we are now able to take the motif
of dreams and of dream interpretation in the story of Joseph
much more seriously than could earlier generations.
Although there is no doubt great danger inherent in this,
and although the bases of the scientific interpretation of
dreams are surely still uncertain, we can nevertheless affirm
with confidence that the subconscious layers of our
humanity that are expressed in dreams are related also to
our conscious and waking humanity, even though we are
largely or even totally unaware of it.

2.   The chief baker and the chief butler

If we put aside for a moment the realization that it is dreams
which are being reported here, we discover in them two
especially lively miniatures from life at the Pharaoh's court
in Egypt. They describe the service of two highly-placed
officials whose work is personal service to the ruler. Like
the abundance of other descriptions of Egyptian life and of

the Egyptian court which occur in the following chapters, these two glimpses grow out of Israel's encounter with Egypt and its interest in that country. This interest harks back to very early encounters with Egypt made by individual groups and tribes in the days before the tribal alliance. It is an interest which was based on the time of the sojourn in Egypt (of only a single group), ending with the exodus, and later reaching new heights in the time of Solomon. Joseph's story is the most lively and literary record we have of Israel's encounter with Egypt.

Here we can see a theme which is theologically very important in the Joseph story. In this entire narrative there is not even the faintest reflection of the Egyptian cult, the grandiose religious doctrines or the highly-developed religious literature. Apparently, all of this did not interest the Israelites in the least at that time. From this we can surmise that the Egyptian religious doctrine and cult in no way tempted Israel. Throughout, the story refers in a matter-of-fact tone to the works of Yahweh, the God of Israel, in Egypt. When Joseph asks the two Egyptian officials, "Do not interpretations belong to God?" it goes without saying that he is speaking about the God who was with him in a land of strangers. The fact that the two officials do not know this God, but serve other powerful gods, is of no importance at all. In this we can see the witness of a strong young faith in which there was not yet any hankering after other gods.

For everything else which there was to see and learn in Egypt, however, the interest of the young Israel was just that much more intense. It was a very lively and alert interest in all things characteristic of the Egyptian empire, such as the political, social and economic conditions which are evident on every page of the story of Joseph. It is therefore clear that a confident and living faith can co-exist with an intellectual and personal interest in a culture which Israel encountered on its way through history. And we can then say that there will be a continuing relation linking Joseph's personal interest in the two imprisoned officials and the objective interest in the life of the Egyptians as well as their institutions, a relation that is present at every point in the story.

In this chapter it is the phenomenon of the Egyptian court officials which piques the interest of the narrator and plays a part in the formation of the narrative. That the Pharaoh has a chief baker and a chief butler in his personal service, that such a high official can, from one day to the next, land in prison because the Pharaoh is angry with him, and that one of them can just as suddenly be restored to his functions and honor, while the other is sent to the gallows (in the narrative beautifully expressed by the play on the verb "to raise up the head") – these are observations which reveal a fascination for the life of the Egyptian court.

3. The forgotten request

To these observations on life in the court of the Pharaoh belongs also the fact that it was possible in this system for an individual simply to perish. Each person is so obsessed with his own downfall and rise that the request of an unfortunate one who has done a good deed can be quickly forgotten. In this detail of Joseph's request to the chief butler to think of him when he once more enjoys Pharaoh's favor, as well as in the laconic concluding remark that the chief butler simply forgot him, it is once more a general human characteristic which comes into the foreground. Here, for the first time in the Bible, we find the consciousness of a human characteristic that asserts itself whenever simple human feelings are suppressed by a hierarchical juxtaposition and interaction of authorities and social classes, as was the case at the Egyptian court. In such a situation, a person can simply be forgotten, and in this forgetting is revealed the threat to human relations which results when the differences between social classes are too great. In this early story we have an anticipation of the strong expression of social thinking which appears in so many places in the Old Testament.

Application

It will not be necessary to say a great deal more about the presentation of this Bible study. The presentation can follow the points in which the interpretation has already been summarized thematically.

In addition, a practical stimulus can be given. When this chapter is explained in a small group, there is a good opportunity here to show examples of the fact that we know more about the Egypt into which Joseph came as a slave, where he rose from prison to be minister of the Pharaoh, than we do about any other people or country of antiquity. This can be illustrated by the use of any book of pictures about Egypt. Every one contains pictures and figures which will directly illustrate for us some aspect of the Joseph story. As an example, I mention "The World of the Egyptians" by W. Wolf in the collection *Great Cultures of Antiquity*, (Stuttgart: 1958). Here, for example, the "model of a house and of a street in Amarna," Figure 74, can give us an impression how the house where Joseph was administrator may have looked. Or the dream of the chief butler comes alive for us through the presentation of the wine harvest in Figure 58. These are but some examples, of which we can find enough in any collection of pictures about Egypt.

4

Joseph's Exaltation (Genesis 41:1–32)

Text

41 *After two whole years, Pharaoh dreamed that he was standing by the Nile, ²and there came up out of the Nile seven sleek and fat cows, and they grazed in the reed grass. ³Then seven other cows, ugly and thin, came up out of the Nile after them, and stood by the other cows on the bank of the Nile. ⁴The ugly and thin cows ate up the seven sleek and fat cows. And Pharaoh awoke. ⁵Then he fell asleep and dreamed a second time; seven ears of grain, plump and good, were growing on one stalk. ⁶Then seven ears, thin and blighted by the east wind, sprouted after them. ⁷The thin ears swallowed up the seven plump and full ears. Pharaoh awoke, and it was a dream. ⁸In the morning his spirit was troubled; so he sent and called for all the magicians of Egypt and all its wise men. Pharaoh told them his dreams, but there was no one who could interpret them to Pharaoh.*

9 Then the chief cupbearer said to Pharaoh, "I remember my faults today. ¹⁰Once Pharaoh was angry with his servants, and put me and the chief baker in custody in the house of the captain of the guard. ¹¹We dreamed on the same night, he and I, each having a dream with its own meaning. ¹²A young Hebrew was there with us, a servant of the captain of the guard. When we told him, he interpreted our dreams to us, giving an interpretation to each according to his dream. ¹³As he interpreted to us, so it turned out; I was restored to my office, and the baker was hanged."

14 Then Pharaoh sent for Joseph, and he was hurriedly brought out of the dungeon. When he had shaved himself and changed his clothes, he came in before Pharaoh. ¹⁵And Pharaoh said to Joseph, "I have had a dream, and there is no one who can interpret it. I have heard it said of you that when you hear a dream you can interpret it." ¹⁶Joseph answered Pharaoh, "It is not I; God will give Pharaoh a favorable answer." ¹⁷Then Pharaoh said to Joseph, "In my dream I was standing on the banks of the Nile; ¹⁸and seven cows, fat and sleek, came up out of the Nile and fed in the reed grass. ¹⁹Then

*seven other cows came up after them, poor, very ugly, and thin.
Never had I seen such ugly ones in all the land of Egypt.* [20]*The thin
and ugly cows ate up the first seven fat cows,* [21]*but when they had
eaten them no one would have known that they had done so, for
they were still as ugly as before. Then I awoke.* [22]*I fell asleep a second
time and I saw in my dream seven ears of grain, full and good,
growing on one stalk,* [23]*and seven ears, withered, thin, and blighted
by the east wind, sprouting after them;* [24]*and the thin ears swallowed
up the seven good ears. But when I told it to the magicians, there
was no one who could explain it to me."*

*25 Then Joseph said to Pharaoh, "Pharaoh's dreams are one and
the same; God has revealed to Pharaoh what he is about to do.*
[26]*The seven good cows are seven years, and the seven good ears
are seven years; the dreams are one.* [27]*The seven lean and ugly
cows that came up after them are seven years, as are the seven
empty ears blighted by the east wind. They are seven years of
famine.* [28]*It is as I told Pharaoh; God has shown to Pharaoh what
he is about to do.* [29]*There will come seven years of great plenty
throughout all the land of Egypt.* [30]*After them there will arise
seven years of famine, and all the plenty will be forgotten in the
land of Egypt; the famine will consume the land.* [31]*The plenty
will no longer be known in the land because of the famine that
will follow, for it will be very grievous.* [32]*And the doubling of
Pharaoh's dream means that the thing is fixed by God, and God
will shortly bring it about.*

In the first part of the chapter, i.e., up to v. 32, there is an
autonomous narrative about Pharaoh's dreams and their
interpretation by Joseph. In its interpretation, it is necessary
always to keep in mind the previous dream interpretation
in chapters 37 and 40. In the loose connection which binds
them together one can note an intensification from the
dreams in chapter 37 to the dreams of Pharaoh in chapter 41.

Structure

1–8	Pharaoh's dreams	
	1–4	The seven cows
	5–7	The ears of grain
	8	The Egyptian wise men cannot interpret them

The narrative is clear and simply organized. It derives its suspense from the failure of the Egyptian wise men to interpret the dreams (vv. 8 and 24b), who are thus put in an unfavorable light. In the middle of the narrative (v. 16), Joseph's successful interpretation is, however, credited to God, the God who is with Joseph. In this way, the middle of the narrative acquires a tone of praise to God. Verse 25 states what it is about God that is praised; Joseph makes known to Pharaoh what God is about to do. As in chapter 40, the announcement is a statement of something which is going to come about. But it has an extra meaning, namely, that the announcement of this event makes it possible for many to encounter the coming event in such a way that it becomes redemptive for them. Here the dream motif is brought into a solid relationship with the theme (chapter 50:20) which interprets the entire story; God guided everything in the Joseph story in such a manner that many people were kept alive by it. The action turns on the dream at the beginning and at the climax. A dream is the occasion for Joseph's fall into disfavor (chapter 37); a dream becomes the occasion for his rise (chapter 41). One dream qualifies the brothers' crime: "As for you, you meant evil against me;" the other dream introduces the saving and preserving action of God even toward those who had planned to do evil: "but God meant it for good." One dream seems to testify to a malicious self-promotion by Joseph; by means of the other dream, which Joseph is empowered to interpret, the first dream is led to fulfillment against all expectations. Through the exaltation of Joseph, God carries through His plan to preserve the family of Jacob.

Interpretation

41:1–8 *Pharaoh's dreams*

In the ancient world, dreams played an important role as a medium of revelation. Though this fact cannot be demonstrated here, I call attention to E. L. Ehrlich's *Der Traum im Alten Testament* (Dreams in the Old Testament) (BZAW 73, 1953), and to a short summary of the same in the article "Traum" in RGG³, Vol. VI. He says here (p. 1002): "A special role is played by the dreams of kings (in Mesopotamia reported by, among others, Ashurbanipal in the 7th Century and Nabonid in the 6th). In the so-called autobiography of the Hittite king Hattusili III in the 13th Century, dreams represent a means by which God shows the king the path to power. The dream of the Egyptian king Thutmose IV at the end of the 15th Century is dreamed in a numinous location in the shadow of the great Sphinx . . ."

Pharaoh's dream in the Joseph story can therefore be seen to correspond entirely to the reality of its time. From the Old Testament we are familiar with the dream of King Solomon (1 Kings 3:5–15), in which Solomon experiences a revelation of God which directly involves his kingdom. In the dreams of kings is revealed the special relationship that they enjoyed with divinity in the ancient world. Also revealed, however, is the immense responsibility they bore toward their people. A king must be provident for his people and his land; their woe or welfare depend in great degree on his foresight, decisions, and deeds.

The dreams of Pharaoh in our narrative are clearly concerned with the economy of the land, the supplying of its people's needs through agriculture (the ears of grain) and cattle-breeding (the cows). To this end, too, the king must exert himself, for also the economy of the land depends on his decisions and plans. And because also in Egypt the dreams of kings can be understood as divine revelations (see the above quotation), the economy of the land is still viewed here in close relationship with divine activities, so that in this case the king is the connecting link between the divine will and the economy of the land.

By means of these dreams of the Pharaoh related in the Joseph story, we can come to understand a process that is significant for world history: as the dominant form of government that had persisted already for many thousands of years, royalty had maintained its vitality through the special relation of the king to the divine, however that might have looked at a given time. The king was, in a special sense, the distributor of divine blessing. In the measure that this relation to the divine was weakened and eventually entirely dissipated, royalty diminished in its significance and power. Here we have the real root of the disappearance of monarchies in favor of democracy.

41:9–16 *Joseph is called before Pharaoh*
The middle section, vv. 9–16, which links the dreams and their meaning, has its goal in the statement of v. 16: "It is not I; God will give Pharaoh a favorable answer." The sentence says, first of all, that the interpretation of the dream is attributable to God, for it is God who qualifies Joseph to interpret the dream, and who has brought him before the Pharaoh on this occasion. At the same time, the statement says that it will be a favorable interpretation which will serve the welfare of the land. This indication from the human being to God, "It is not I; God will give Pharaoh a favorable answer" presents praise of God in narrative form which gives the honor to God for his activity in relation to human beings. He is the one who leads the confused and erring ways of humans to a good conclusion.

And so even in a modest, all-too human event, the quiet rule of God can be perceived; the chief butler, who had completely forgotten Joseph, is reminded by the dreams of Pharaoh. Now he is able even to call attention to himself and give Pharaoh an important orientation! But the chief butler's remembering stands against a background of the failure of the Egyptian wise men, who were not able to interpret the dream (vv. 8b and 24b). Therein is reflected the other side of the praise of God. In the Psalms, God is praised as the Lord of history, which means that he really knows what has happened and can announce that which is to come. What the fortune tellers and wise men of Egypt cannot do, that is given to the Hebrew slave, because the God before whom everything which happens lies open is with him. Further, our narrative intends to say that he is the same God who surveys the great, wide world and rules

over it, so that he can show Pharaoh in Egypt how a famine
can be avoided, and who is with the anonymous Hebrew
slave and guides his steps. He has guided things so that
these two so different worlds encounter one another when
Joseph goes before Pharaoh.

41:17–32   *Joseph interprets Pharaoh's dreams*
In the dreams of the two officials, the point is simply the
announcement of the fate which each of them will have.
This is consistent with the purely preparatory function
which the two have in the narrative as a whole. They serve
to explain why the Pharaoh summoned a Hebrew slave to
interpret his dreams. The dreams, however, are more than
just announcement. Their aim is to give an instruction
which, though not contained in the dream itself, will be a
profound intervention in the historical process. In
comparison to chapter 40 (and also chapter 37) we have in
chapter 41 a decided increase of the authority and the
meaning attributed to the dream.

It is noteworthy that the dreams appear always in pairs.
It is obviously part of the art of dream interpretation that
the relationship of both halves of the pair to one another
must be determined. While the seemingly similar dreams
of the two officials require contrasting interpretations,
Joseph says of the two dreams of the Pharaoh "It is one and
the same dream," and both dreams have the same meaning.
Behind this striking feature there is clearly a well-developed
art of dream interpretation alluded to here.

An astonishing fidelity to reality is revealed in the
comparison of the two repetitions of the dreams of Pharaoh
in vv. 1–7 and 17–24. Although they agree as to the facts
involved, the second version differs characteristically from
the first in that it emphasizes as the main point that it is
presenting a reflection of the dreamer about a characteristic
of his dream, and that it is a little exaggerated. The narrator
is aware that such a report will necessarily come out a little
differently when it is told the second time. Just in what
direction it customarily tends to differ is masterfully
understood here.

When we carefully examine Joseph's interpretation of
the dream we discover how amazingly detailed and many-
sided it is:

Verse 25. Interpretation of the kind of dream. Both dreams have the same purpose, which is to announce what God means to do.

Verses 26–27. Interpretation of the components of the action of the dream.

Verse 28. The meaning of the dream (= v. 25)

Verses 29–30. Interpretation of the events of the dream:

> There will come seven years . . .
> after them there will arise seven years . . .

Verse 32. Interpretation of the doubling of the dream.

Two differing kinds of interpretation distinguish themselves. In vv. 26–27 individual details are interpreted, which is clearly reminiscent of the allegorical method of interpretation. In vv. 29–30, on the other hand, the event of the dream is translated into the area of actual history, which is a fundamentally different way of interpreting. And it thereby becomes evident that in vv. 29–30 (and in v. 32, which belongs with it) the first traces of prophetic language are discernible. The beginning of v. 29 is reminiscent of the frequently recurring introduction to a prophetic word: "Behold, days will come when . . ." The description of the famine in v. 30b evidences parallelism of structure (as also v. 32b) and is reminiscent of announcements of disaster in words of the prophets. Verse 32b should be compared with Isaiah 28:22: "for I have heard a decree of destruction from the LORD GOD of hosts upon the whole world," and with Isaiah 5:19: "let the plan of the Holy One of Israel hasten to fulfillment." All of this shows clearly that we have here a very early joining of dream interpretation and prophetic discourse. In both of them the concern was to announce that which God would do, and such announcement was evidently already existent before the appearance of prophetism. In this connection it is important that early prophetism in Israel directed its words primarily to the kings, as we see when the announcement contained in the Pharaoh's dream becomes a message directed to the king.

Application

The interpretation has shown that the statement in v. 16 is of central importance in this section, and that it is borne up by the praise of God, the God who in his majesty is the Lord of everything which happens and can therefore show how to defend against famine in Egypt, the praise of the God who has mercy on the sufferer and lifts him out of the depths (Psalms 113).

The task is to relate this theological center of the section in a clear and natural manner to everything else which happens here, including even the meaning of the seven fat and the seven lean years for the Egyptian economy. That can be accomplished by following the three points of the interpretation.

(1) The dreams of Pharaoh should be interpreted according to the two directions presented here: (a) The special relation to God attributed to the king in the ancient world, that included also the possibility that he could be the recipient of a specific word of God about his royal responsibilities (1 Kings 3); (b) The high responsibility which the king once possessed in that the welfare and woes of the land depended on his decisions and acts. Because of this text, we have an opportunity to understand in its wider horizons the meaning of royalty in the ancient world, why the king had such a high position in both testaments of the Bible, and why Jesus of Nazareth himself was given the title of king (Christos).

(2) Before the Pharaoh, Joseph speaks the word which defines the narrative (v. 16). Here it will be necessary to bring to expression in both directions (see above) the praise of God which stands behind the narrative. The story makes it easy for us to see the portrayal, in the two figures of Pharaoh and of the Hebrew slave, these two forms of God's action. When Joseph comes before Pharaoh, both come together, and when here an insignificant and inconsequential event like the friendly interest in two prisoners can become the occasion for a far-reaching change in the history of the Egyptian empire, it reflects this very inclusiveness of God's action, "who is seated on high, who looks far down on the heavens and the earth" (Psalm 113).

(3) The dream interpretation here directs attention to the question about God's word and activity, for which there is an unlimited abundance of possibilities. The decisive issue here is not the dream interpretation itself, but rather the abundance of possibilities of "interpretation," all of which are based on the certainty which Joseph expresses in v. 16. Here there is an opportunity to show, based on Joseph's dream interpretation, how greatly the interest in God's word and God's will necessarily fluctuate at various times, and how there is nevertheless a continuity that extends from this interpretation of dreams through the complex history of the interpretation of the word of God down to our own days.

5

Joseph's Exaltation and Duties in Egypt
(Genesis 41:33–57)

Text

³³*"Now therefore let Pharaoh select a man who is discerning and wise, and set him over the land of Egypt. ³⁴Let Pharaoh proceed to appoint overseers over the land, and take one-fifth of the produce of the land of Egypt during the seven plenteous years. ³⁵Let them gather all the food of these good years that are coming, and lay up grain under the authority of Pharaoh for food in the cities, and let them keep it. ³⁶That food shall be a reserve for the land against the seven years of famine that are to befall the land of Egypt, so that the land may not perish through the famine."*

37 The proposal pleased Pharaoh and all his servants. ³⁸Pharaoh said to his servants, "Can we find anyone else like this – one in whom is the spirit of God?" ³⁹So Pharaoh said to Joseph, "Since God has shown you all this, there is no one so discerning and wise as you. ⁴⁰You shall be over my house, and all my people shall order themselves as you command; only with regard to the throne will I be greater than you." ⁴¹And Pharaoh said to Joseph, "See, I have set you over all the land of Egypt." ⁴²Removing his signet ring from his hand, Pharaoh put it on Joseph's hand; he arrayed him in garments of fine linen, and put a gold chain around his neck. ⁴³He had him ride in the chariot of his second-in-command; and they cried out in front of him, "Bow the knee!" Thus he set him over all the land of Egypt. ⁴⁴Moreover Pharaoh said to Joseph, "I am Pharaoh, and without your consent no one shall lift up hand or foot in all the land of Egypt." ⁴⁵Pharaoh gave Joseph the name Zaphenathpaneah; and he gave him Asenath daughter of Potiphera, priest of On, as his wife. Thus Joseph gained authority over the land of Egypt.

46 Joseph was thirty years old when he entered the service of Pharaoh king of Egypt. And Joseph went out from the presence of Pharaoh, and went through all the land of Egypt. ⁴⁷During the seven plenteous years the earth produced abundantly. ⁴⁸He gathered up all the food

*of the seven years when there was plenty in the land of Egypt, and
stored up food in the cities; he stored up in every city the food from
the fields around it.* [49]*So Joseph stored up grain in such abundance
– like the sand of the sea – that he stopped measuring it; it was
beyond measure.*

*50 Before the years of famine came, Joseph had two sons, whom
Asenath daughter of Potiphera, priest of On, bore to him.* [51]*Joseph
named the first-born Manasseh, "For," he said, "God has made me
forget all my hardship and all my father's house."* [52]*The second he
named Ephraim, "For God has made me fruitful in the land of my
misfortunes."*

*53 The seven years of plenty that prevailed in the land of Egypt
came to an end;* [54]*and the seven years of famine began to come, just
as Joseph had said. There was famine in every country, but
throughout the land of Egypt there was bread.* [55]*When all the land
of Egypt was famished, the people cried to Pharaoh for bread.
Pharaoh said to all the Egyptians, "Go to Joseph; what he says to
you, do."* [56]*And since the famine had spread over all the land, Joseph
opened all the storehouses, and sold to the Egyptians, for the famine
was severe in the land of Egypt.* [57]*Moreover, all the world came to
Joseph in Egypt to buy grain, because the famine became severe
throughout the world.*

Structure

33–36	Joseph's counsel to Pharaoh
37–46	Joseph is installed as plenipotentiary
37–41	Joseph is named as executor
42–44	Investiture and installation in office
45–46	A new name and an Egyptian wife
47–57	Joseph at his duties: prevention of famine

Interpretation

While the first part of chapter 41 has a clear theological
center in v. 16, the second part moves into conclusions which
belong entirely to that which is worldly and human. This is
clearly labelled; the instruction which Joseph gives in his

counsel to the Pharaoh is no longer a divine message but rather human deliberation. Although based on what had been made known by God in the dream, it is distinguished from it as a plan of the human spirit, which is encouraged to project its own plan. Clearly evident here is an attitude which assigns high value to human planning and reckons with the possibilities which can be achieved by human beings. In this it is entirely in harmony with the intellectual world in which the Joseph narrative originated.

In the description which follows, we once more need to see above all the reflection on and the working out of an historical encounter, that of the young Israel – or of a group within it – with the Egyptian empire, and more precisely with the economic institutions of this realm. When we think of the initial situation, which is that of semi-nomads surprised by famine who attempt to obtain grain in Egypt, it becomes clear what a deep impression must have been made on them by this totally new and unfamiliar form of economic planning, which was typified most conspicuously by the the great granaries which they saw as soon as they entered the country. It is well to keep in mind that it is this encounter which provides the historical background of this section. This does not, however, mean that what is described is historically correct in every respect. It is not true that the economic planning described here was something new. Long before the time described by our narrative, government granaries had been features of ancient Egypt. The large-scale management of grain surpluses – which for Egypt had long been a familiar feature of the great empire and a reality without which life in this complicated society would have become unthinkable – was something astonishingly great and wonderful for the wandering tribes who were seeing it for the first time. It is a meditation on this phenomenon which is reflected in our story.

The first thing that Israel thought and said about this was that such a wonderful institution could come only from God. Certainly it is based on the planning and industry of human beings. But somewhere behind the human planning and activity must stand the activity of God. And it is just this which our narrative says; this planned economy is profoundly related to the plan of God, who also works through human means and human projects "to support

many people." It becomes evident here how much power
the praise of God had in Israel. This incident, which was
really so distant and removed from God's action among
his people, must belong in some way to the activity of the
God who is the saving and preserving one "who gives food
to all flesh." Even the management of surplus grain in Egypt
had to be based, finally, on the life-preserving activity of
God. And that is revealed – so says the narrative – precisely
at the point where by means of this storage of surplus grain
a group of individuals who belong to God's people are
saved from starvation.

At the same time, however, the narrative stresses that all
of this happened by means which were entirely natural and
rational; it was the rational aspect of the policy of storing
grain which receives emphasis here. Our story is therefore
a very significant attempt, based on Israel's praise of God,
to reconcile with the activity of God such phenomena as
Egypt's policy of grain storage. Though that may be a rather
fumbling and naive attempt, at least from our point of view,
what is significant is that Israel's praise of God should
extend itself so far. In this attempt there was present a living
interest in the life processes of the surrounding world. This
is one of the very few contexts in the Bible in which
significant economic processes are linked with the activity
of God. One insight which emerges clearly is significant
also for us – although the economic processes are here seen
in the context of God's activity, this does not in any sense
obscure their being perceived as independent and
autonomous processes, within which human planning and
rational design find their place.

Joseph as Egyptian plenipotentiary

That which in this entire Joseph narrative seems to us least
probable and most like a fairy tale – namely, that a Hebrew
slave, one who had been confined in Pharaoh's prison, could
have received from him such a high and responsible office
– precisely this is historically entirely possible. Gunkel
comments "That Canaanite slaves received high positions
in Egypt is true; the pharaohs of the new realm chose their
ministers among the slaves of their house, who were often
foreigners." Egyptologists, too, have repeatedly said that
such an event was entirely plausible.

From Pharaoh's point of view, what Joseph brought to his high position was his wisdom, which was reflected in his counsel and recognized by the Pharaoh in his ability to interpret the dream. At the point of Joseph's elevation, the narrator speaks of wisdom in a way which is interventive and prescriptive. I refer here once more to the document by von Rad which examines the influence of wisdom on the Joseph narrative and which provides the clearest case of the exaltation of wisdom. For our contemporary understanding it is especially important that we see the entirely tranquil combination of the fear of God and of wisdom as it is understood here ("the fear of the Lord is the beginning of wisdom"). God is with Joseph; this presence of God is validated in the gift of dream interpretation, but also equally so in the wisdom of Joseph, and that means here in his worldly wisdom, especially in his political and economic capacity in worldly matters. As the wisdom of a king in Israel is understood as the result of the blessing of God, so this wisdom expresses itself in competence in both external and internal politics. The relation of wisdom to blessing is understood in this way; blessing is the power to grow. The blessing of growth shores up both bodily and spiritual powers, and wisdom is something which has grown and matured. In the case of Joseph, therefore, there is an intimate relation between his talent for dream interpretation and his wisdom, "Since God has shown you all this, there is no one so discerning and wise as you" (v. 39).

Wisdom, however, although it is understood as a gift of the blessing of God, is not as such restricted by the boundaries of the people of God. Such wisdom is to be found everywhere on the earth, and in Israel, too, one can learn from the wisdom of other peoples, as the collection of the Proverbs shows. When Joseph applies his God-given wisdom in a position at the Egyptian court, that is thoroughly consistent with the possibilities inherent in wisdom. Although wisdom is above all suited to the king, it is also one of the elements of life at the court which is given special attention. Based on this we can understand why our narrator sees no difficulty in placing Joseph so thoroughly within the ceremony of the Egyptian court, or in permitting Joseph to be so Egyptian that he even receives

an Egyptian name and an Egyptian wife. The court
ceremonies are, of course, shot through with cultic elements,
and a certain participation in religiously-conditioned
solemnities must certainly be unavoidable for Joseph. Our
narrator, however, sees life at court characterized much
more by wisdom, a wisdom not limited to any one nation
or religion.

Joseph's family

In spite of everything, however, the narrator was clearly
concerned to tell his hearers that Joseph in his new
responsibilities and in his new glory continued to be a part
of the history out of which he comes, committed also to the
God who was with him through everything. He says this
in an entirely unobtrusive way, without departing from the
flow of the story when he includes information about
Joseph's family in the genealogies of the patriarchs (vv. 50–
52):

> Before the years of famine came, Joseph had two sons,
> whom Asenath daughter of Potiphera priest of On bore
> to him. Joseph named the first-born Manasseh, "For,"
> he said, "God has made me forget all my hardship and
> all my father's house." The second he named Ephraim,
> "For God has made me fruitful in the land of my
> misfortunes."

The names of these two sons of Joseph are firmly rooted in
the tradition which the narrator cites here. The
interpretations which Joseph gives for the names of his two
sons are so far removed from their literal meaning that they
can really not be taken as explanations of names at all. The
narrator intends rather by these interpretations to say what
Joseph's children mean to him there in his new situation in
exile. Both interpretations are praise of God. In both of the
statements, God is praised as savior from trouble and as
One who blesses and causes to flourish. To the listening
ear, these two statements interpret the entire story of Joseph
as an activity of God for which Joseph can offer praise. By
means of his exaltation and of the great responsibility into
which he had been thrust, God had made him forget every
hardship. And when "and all my father's house" is

included, that is to be understood in the sense of all the suffering that his relatives had brought upon him. While the interpretation of the first name looks backward, the second looks to the future; "God has made me fruitful in the land of my misfortunes." In the place where he had to pass through so many difficulties, there God had given him a new beginning in his children.

In the area of his life and his family, Joseph remains indissolubly bound, as if nothing had happened, with the God of his fathers and with the actions of this God. In this area the praise of God continues alive, and the names of the children are a silent witness that the activity of the God of the fathers is being passed on to the children.

Application

The point of departure could be the situation in which most Christians find themselves today, that is that daily life plays itself out in a realm in which there is absolutely no perception of or contact with God's activity and word. A similar situation prevails in our narrative, although under totally different conditions.

From this starting point one can describe that particular reality with which our story deals, namely, economics. One can make reference to the business sections of our newspapers and to the powerful and many-sided, autonomous reality of business in our times which they reflect. When we encounter there the concept of economic planning, which occurs often enough, then we have arrived directly at our text. For economic planning is the content of Joseph's counsel to Pharaoh.

We can then think about the wisdom which qualifies Joseph as a counselor and administrator, the wisdom which even as worldly wisdom can be understood as a gift of blessing and of the presence of God. That Joseph is granted the powers to avert a serious famine is, on first view, simply a wise and well-planned economic policy. More profoundly it is related to the fact that God, in acting through the wisdom of a gifted person, desires to preserve the life of many people.

Joseph's ability to be entirely at the disposition of a heathen court, where he no doubt had to "go along" with many things, and yet at the same time could hold fast with great naturalness to his faith, deserves our attention. This situation offers a possibility of addressing our own situation today, without necessarily drawing explicit parallels. But it can also stimulate us to think about how the components of our modern life, which appear to be so absolutely self-directed, can, when considered more profoundly, be seen in relation to that totality that is in God's hand.

6

The First Journey of the Brothers to Egypt (Genesis 42)

Text

42 When Jacob learned that there was grain in Egypt, he said to his sons, "Why do you keep looking at one another? ²I have heard," he said, "that there is grain in Egypt; go down and buy grain for us there, that we may live and not die." ³So ten of Joseph's brothers went down to buy grain in Egypt. ⁴But Jacob did not send Joseph's brother Benjamin with his brothers, for he feared that harm might come to him. ⁵Thus the sons of Israel were among the other people who came to buy grain, for the famine had reached the land of Canaan.

6 Now Joseph was governor over the land; it was he who sold to all the people of the land. And Joseph's brothers came and bowed themselves before him with their faces to the ground. ⁷When Joseph saw his brothers, he recognized them, but he treated them like strangers and spoke harshly to them. "Where do you come from?" he said. They said, "From the land of Canaan, to buy food." ⁸Although Joseph had recognized his brothers, they did not recognize him. ⁹Joseph also remembered the dreams that he had dreamed about them. He said to them, "You are spies; you have come to see the nakedness of the land!" ¹⁰They said to him, "No, my lord; your servants have come to buy food. ¹¹We are all sons of one man; we are honest men; your servants have never been spies." ¹²But he said to them, "No, you have come to see the nakedness of the land!" ¹³They said, "We, your servants, are twelve brothers, the sons of a certain man in the land of Canaan; the youngest, however, is now with our father, and one is no more." ¹⁴But Joseph said to them, "It is just as I have said to you; you are spies! ¹⁵Here is how you shall be tested: as Pharaoh lives, you shall not leave this place unless your youngest brother comes here! ¹⁶Let one of you go and bring your brother, while the rest of you remain in prison, in order that your words may be tested, whether there is truth in you; or else, as

61

Pharaoh lives, surely you are spies." [17] *And he put them all together in prison for three days.*

18 On the third day Joseph said to them, *"Do this and you will live, for I fear God:* [19] *if you are honest men, let one of your brothers stay here where you are imprisoned. The rest of you shall go and carry grain for the famine of your households,* [20] *and bring your youngest brother to me. Thus your words will be verified, and you shall not die."* And they agreed to do so. [21] They said to one another, *"Alas, we are paying the penalty for what we did to our brother; we saw his anguish when he pleaded with us, but we would not listen. That is why this anguish has come upon us."* [22] Then Reuben answered them, *"Did I not tell you not to wrong the boy? But you would not listen. So now there comes a reckoning for his blood."* [23] They did not know that Joseph understood them, since he spoke with them through an interpreter. [24] He turned away from them and wept; then he returned and spoke to them. And he picked out Simeon and had him bound before their eyes. [25] Joseph then gave orders to fill their bags with grain, to return every man's money to his sack, and to give them provisions for their journey. This was done for them.

26 They loaded their donkeys with their grain, and departed. [27] When one of them opened his sack to give his donkey fodder at the lodging place, he saw his money at the top of the sack. [28] He said to his brothers, *"My money has been put back; here it is in my sack!"* At this they lost heart and turned trembling to one another, saying, *"What is this that God has done to us?"*

29 When they came to their father Jacob in the land of Canaan, they told him all that had happened to them, saying, [30] *"The man, the lord of the land, spoke harshly to us, and charged us with spying on the land.* [31] *But we said to him, 'We are honest men, we are not spies.* [32] *We are twelve brothers, sons of our father; one is no more, and the youngest is now with our father in the land of Canaan.'* [33] *Then the man, the lord of the land, said to us, 'By this I shall know that you are honest men: leave one of your brothers with me, take grain for the famine of your households, and go your way.* [34] *Bring your youngest brother to me, and I shall know that you are not spies but honest men. Then I will release your brother to you, and you may trade in the land.'"*

35 As they were emptying their sacks, there in each one's sack was his bag of money. When they and their father saw their bundles of money, they were dismayed. [36] And their father Jacob said to them, *"I am the one you have bereaved of children: Joseph is no more, and Simeon is no more, and now you would take Benjamin. All this has happened to me!"* [37] Then Reuben said to his father, *"You may kill*

my two sons if I do not bring him back to you. Put him in my
hands, and I will bring him back to you." ³⁸But he said, "My son
shall not go down with you, for his brother is dead, and he alone is
left. If harm should come to him on the journey that you are to
make, you would bring down my gray hairs with sorrow to Sheol."

Structure

1–6a   Departure of the brothers

    1b .   The father's challenge.

    3   The brothers depart without Benjamin

    6a   Connecting passage: Joseph sells grain in
              Egypt

6b–26   The encounter in Egypt

Recognition

    6b   The brothers throw themselves at Joseph's
              feet

    8–9a   Joseph recognizes them and remembers
              the dreams

Accusation

    9b   You are spies!

    11b, 13   Defense

    14–16   Demand for verification of identity

The Prison

    17   Into prison for three days

    18–20   One must remain behind

The Recognition

    21   Recognition ". . . therefore is this disaster
              come upon us."

    22   Reuben: Did I not tell you!

    23–24a   Joseph weeps – and binds Simeon

Interpretation

In chapter 42 we finally have the convergence of the two
narrative lines – the inner and the outer – which have been
approaching each other from the very beginning. The
narration returns to the family of Jacob at the beginning of
the chapter, and throughout there is a contrasting of the
two different spheres of action; Jacob's family and the
Egyptian plenipotentiary in his province of power. The
"inner" narrative line is reattached to the story when the
events of the crime which had apparently ended the
brothers' relation to Joseph reappear as present reality. That
is expressed in chapter 42 by means of the two kinds of
perception; Joseph recognizes his brothers, but they do not
know him. Through that which happens to them they
probably do understand, however, that the injury
committed against their brother has once more become a
present fact: "... that is why this anguish is come upon us."
It is this reciprocal but divergent "understanding" which
determines this entire section of the narrative. Thereby the
narrator calls attention, though without explicitly saying
so, to the one who brings the brothers back together in this
double sense.

42: 1–6a *Departure of the brothers*
Famine is the cause of the next stage of events. This is one
of the most significant motifs in the life of the semi-nomads

during the patriarchal era (see Genesis 12). It was extremely important, for life and death were in the balance. One possibility was to buy grain in one of the great agricultural countries, although, as our story illustrates, this could involve the greatest kind of risk. This attempt could cost either one's freedom or one's very life. It was for this reason that the father had to urge action, for the brothers knew what could be waiting for them there. Right at the beginning the similarity to the initial situation is apparent. Once again there is a confrontation between the father and the brothers, the subject being the youngest brother, Benjamin, whom his father will not permit to go along. And once more, in this initial situation are the seeds of the conflict which then unfolds.

42: 6b–26   The encounter in Egypt

Verses 6b, 8, 9a. "[A]nd bowed themselves before him with their faces to the ground." This is the very first movement, the first gesture of the encounter, which reveals what the purchase of grain in Egypt means for the brothers. They do not come as buyers in the normal sense. With their request they are rather falling into the sphere of power of an unknown world before whose rulers they are powerless. Before the request for food comes the gesture of subordination, the prostration before the powerful, an act hateful to the free bedouins. In this simple story we have the statement of a characteristic of human co-existence which, in one form or another, has always recurred right down to the present day – that for the sake of bread, of food, human beings must bow down before other human beings who have control over that which can save the hungry from death. The action of throwing oneself down expresses better than words what kind of possibilities were implicit in the tension that existed between the powerless hungry and the powerful who controlled the food.

This situation is then affected, however, by an entirely different series of events, for in this case the powerful man is also a brother. For him, the prostration of the brothers is the continuation of an entirely different story, one which began in the father's house when he as a little boy told his dreams to his brothers, "Joseph also remembered the dreams that he had dreamed about them." How will it be possible for these two spheres of activity, which are so different from one another, to encounter one another, coalesce, and achieve agreement?

Verses 9b–13. The dream has come true. The brothers lie on the earth before Joseph and are at his mercy. He now would have the opportunity to take revenge on them. That which follows, however, can only be understood in the sense that Joseph, as soon as he had recognized his brothers, was resolved to try to apply healing to the breach. That cannot happen, however, unless the brothers, for their part, are first brought to "perception." This is the reason that Joseph permits them to experience the full harshness of what it means to be at the mercy of the mighty. The narrator means to say here that pardon at this point immediately after the arrival of the brothers could not have led to a genuine solution. What had happened was too serious for that. The brothers, therefore, are aware of only one aspect of the action; they are in the hands of the mighty. And the blow falls immediately, they are accused of espionage.

Behind this lies another experience from ancient times. In those days it often happened that a small group might, for a variety of reasons, enter foreign territory without anyone being concerned about it. Here, however, they have the new experience of a closed national border, whose violation could cost them freedom or life itself. The accusation of espionage represents the most extreme reaction to such crossing of boundaries. The traveler who innocently goes his way through a certain area is accused of spying with an unfriendly purpose. This represents the first experiences of deadly peril because of the borders which have been established between the lands of settled residents. The brothers probably know that they are powerless in the face of this accusation. How are they to prove that they are not spies? They respond by stating the only thing that would prove that they are not spies if it is believed. To us, the defense of v. 13, "We, your servants, are twelve brothers, the sons of a certain man . . ." does not seem entirely significant. In this situation it is, however, the only argument they have left. What they are saying is that they are members of a familial alliance, not a political one.

An unfriendly action against Egypt by a family group would make no sense. The argument of the brothers demonstrates that our narrative reflects the experience of the encounter of the family group with political powers.

Verses 14–17. Their claim to be "honest men" is of little avail. The foreign official persists in his accusations. Nonetheless, he then involves himself in their defense by demanding that they prove their claim to be a family by producing their youngest brother. This action of his is a clue to turns of events yet to come and which the brothers can not even suspect. At this stage, they are experiencing nothing but naked power. For the third time the accusation is raised against them, and they are thrown into prison.

Verses 18–20. What the brothers now go through is the experience, typical down to our own day, of the powerless in the face of the powerful. The brothers have lain in prison for three days, and are unsure what is to happen to them. After three days they receive another order. It is a further step toward their freedom, and it is expressly described as such, "Do this and you will live . . ." This only plunges them into deeper despair, for to them the changing statements of punishment reveal only their lost condition. Perhaps the mighty one will decide differently after another hour, and so destroy any hope which might present itself. So the will of the powerless is broken. When the mighty one explains the amelioration of their punishment by saying "for I fear God," the brothers are only able to understand that it was the god of the powerful who is helping him to trample the powerless in the dust. Only much later will they understand that Joseph is here referring to that God who will rescue them.

Verses 21–22. We could not begin to track down all the nuances of this story. At this point, the story is gradually working its way to the moment of crisis. In v. 16 the brothers had been told: "Let one of you go and bring your brother . . ." In v. 19, it was "let one of your brothers stay here where you are imprisoned." Once again, the whole process is set in motion before the brothers' eyes. They are free to leave, but one brother has fallen into suffering, and the father is at home. It is for this reason that understanding breaks through at this point:

They said to one another:

"Alas, we are paying the penalty of what we did to our brother; we saw his anguish when he pleaded with us, but we would not listen. That is why this anguish has come upon us."

Here is simply and clearly stated what the Bible means by conversion. It does not happen in an isolated area of pious reflection, but instead in the place where a person faces reality. That is what is happening here. That the brothers are in fear of death and in deadly anxiety has already been reflected clearly enough in the words of Joseph in the above-cited statement and in the following, "and you shall not die." Here the brothers themselves express it. They find a meaning in their anxiety, a meaning that they also relate to that anxiety, and that is the fear of death. They once plunged their own brother into this fear; now the same pitilessness that they once showed him is crushing them. Out of this grows the conviction "Alas, we are paying the penalty for what we did to our brother."

The confession of sin has a liberating effect, and it opens up new possibilities. That is the meaning of the confession of sin which results from free personal insight. The situation of the brothers is at first not at all changed because of this confession of guilt. Something, however, has changed. That which drove them into deadly anxiety and held them there was the strange superior power which is beyond all justice and which menaced them like a monster out after prey. Now they have found some meaning in this anxiety and this threat of death. Now it is no longer simply the Egyptian official who personifies the power of Egypt. The great power has now become only an instrument behind which stands the one who is retributing their own deed.

Verses 23–24. Joseph has heard the conversation of the brothers and must cry. This weeping means that now something has begun to move, and something has changed! His emotion does not, however, hinder him from continuing to be hard to the brothers and to carry on the events which have brought the brothers to their insight. Now they will have to suffer that which has set their guilt in motion. Simeon is bound before the eyes of the others, and the others

know that they will have to inform their father of the loss
of another son.

Verses 25–26. Joseph's command shows the same mixture
of punishment and pardon of his previous acts. The
narrative shows how his acts lead step by step to a
transformation of this tension into a forgiving solution. In
spite of the shadow that lies over this return, the brothers
do bring along the grain by means of which they, their
wives, and their children can be saved from starvation: "that
many people should be kept alive" (Genesis 50:20).

42: 29–37   Return of the brothers

This third part has its high point in the lament of the father
in v. 36:

> And their father Jacob said to them, "I am the one you
> have bereaved of children: Joseph is no more, and
> Simeon is no more, and now you would take Benjamin.
> All this has happened to me."

In order to understand this lament, it is necessary to perceive
that in it an ancient motif of the history of the patriarchs
breaks through the more modern form of the Joseph
narrative and appears here with exactly the same purpose
as if it were a part of the story of Abraham. It is the bitter
pain of the father who has lost his children or is about to
lose them that marks these words. It is the extremely old
understanding that a man lives on in his children, and when
his child dies, it is like a fatal wound for him.

Here all the complicated plot events produced by the
encounter with Egypt are far away. There is nothing left
but the elemental lament of the father. In the dynamics of
the narrative, this sentence places us once more in the
atmosphere of chapter 37, where the narrative had taken
place exclusively in the family. The last verse, too, needs to
be heard against this background. Reuben gives security
for the son who is still in Egypt and for the one who has yet
to go there, "put him in my hands, and I will bring him
back to you." In this guarantee of Reuben's the narrator
means to express that something has really changed. The
brothers' confession has borne fruit. In relation to the father,
too, something has changed. The confession of guilt has

actually had a liberating effect. The father's complaint finds an echo, and the children that the father has lost have now become more important to the brothers than their own rights. Something has changed.

Application

On the basis of this text, one can explain something essential about the acts of God to the people of our times who, in the depths of their hearts, are no longer able to believe in God.

We begin with the concluding lament of the father. Every person can understand it; everyone can hear such words, or say them himself. During all the millennia, nothing has changed in the affliction of a father or a mother who has lost a child or several children. Another thing which has not changed is how difficult or even impossible it is to speak a word of effective consolation in the midst of such grief. That, too, everyone can understand.

Now we compare the lament of the father in 37:34 with that in chapter 42. There is no difference in his grief in the two passages, but there is a difference in the reaction of his sons to the lament. Although they had wanted to comfort him also in chapter 37, in chapter 42 their attitude toward him has become fundamentally different. Something has changed.

The turning point is the realization in v. 21. How does it come about? There is an encounter here of the two directions which have formed the life of the brothers. They loaded themselves down with guilt, then went on with their lives as if nothing had happened. And since everything went on as usual, it looked as if they were going to be able simply to cover up the offense, and go on. Then, however, events came about in the external flux of their lives, in which powerful and uncontrollable forces came into play. First came the famine, then the arbitrary actions of the mighty ruler whom they needed to ask for food. These events led them back to the other continuity which had broken off. Moved by the impression of that which happened to them, they looked back at that event and began really to understand what they had done at that time. At first this was of no help at all to

· them, and changed nothing in their situation. One thing, however, had been changed – they had discovered a structure and a purpose in their life (conversion). Nothing is said about God through all of this. But the narrator of this story does want to say something about the activity of God, and it speaks to our existence when we, at any point, can perceive that there is coherence and meaning in our life. Here the point of recognition has to do with the confession of sin. It has a liberating effect. It frees the brothers from the stifling weight of the meaningless fate which had befallen them in the form of an unknown power. They are now able to see meaning in it because they find a link with another sequence of events in their life. This new meaning which has thereby come into their existence does not look only backward, but forward, and new possibilities are thereby opened for them. That is implied in the word of Reuben at the end (v. 37). Reuben has now come to understand also the grief of the father in a new way. This is reflected in his words, which are no longer merely condolence, but an offer of devotion. A real change has come about, and in this there is testimony to the quiet actions of God.

7

The Second Journey of the Brothers to Egypt (Genesis 43)

Text

43 Now the famine was severe in the land. ²And when they had eaten up the grain that they had brought from Egypt, their father said to them, "Go again, buy us a little more food." ³But Judah said to him, "The man solemnly warned us, saying, 'You shall not see my face unless your brother is with you.' ⁴If you will send our brother with us, we will go down and buy you food; ⁵but if you will not send him, we will not go down, for the man said to us, 'You shall not see my face, unless your brother is with you.'" ⁶Israel said, "Why did you treat me so badly as to tell the man that you had another brother?" ⁷They replied, "The man questioned us carefully about ourselves and our kindred, saying, 'Is your father still alive? Have you another brother?' What we told him was in answer to these questions. Could we in any way know that he would say, 'Bring your brother down'?" ⁸Then Judah said to his father Israel, "Send the boy with me, and let us be on our way, so that we may live and not die – you and we and also our little ones. ⁹I myself will be surety for him; you can hold me accountable for him. If I do not bring him back to you and set him before you, then let me bear the blame forever. ¹⁰If we had not delayed, we would now have returned twice."

11 Then their father Israel said to them, "If it must be so, then do this: take some of the choice fruits of the land in your bags, and carry them down as a present to the man ‑ a little balm and a little honey, gum, resin, pistachio nuts, and almonds. ¹²Take double the money with you. Carry back with you the money that was returned in the top of your sacks; perhaps it was an oversight. ¹³Take your brother also, and be on your way again to the man; ¹⁴may God Almighty grant you mercy before the man, so that he may send back your other brother and Benjamin. As for me, if I am bereaved of my children, I am bereaved." ¹⁵So the men took the present, and

*they took double the money with them, as well as Benjamin. Then
they went on their way down to Egypt, and stood before Joseph.*

16 When Joseph saw Benjamin with them, he said to the steward of
his house, *"Bring the men into the house, and slaughter an animal
and make ready, for the men are to dine with me at noon."* [17]*The
man did as Joseph said, and brought the men to Joseph's house.*
[18]*Now the men were afraid because they were brought to Joseph's
house, and they said, "It is because of the money, replaced in our
sacks the first time, that we have been brought in, so that he may
have an opportunity to fall upon us, to make slaves of us and take
our donkeys."* [19]*So they went up to the steward of Joseph's house
and spoke with him at the entrance to the house.* [20]*They said, "Oh,
my lord, we came down the first time to buy food;* [21]*and when we
came to the lodging place we opened our sacks, and there was each
one's money in the top of his sack, our money in full weight. So we
have brought it back with us.* [22]*Moreover we have brought down
with us additional money to buy food. We do not know who put
our money in our sacks."* [23]*He replied, "Rest assured, do not be
afraid; your God and the God of your father must have put treasure
in your sacks for you; I received your money." Then he brought
Simeon out to them.* [24]*When the steward had brought the men into
Joseph's house, and given them water, and they had washed their
feet, and when he had given their donkeys fodder,* [25]*they made the
present ready for Joseph's coming at noon, for they had heard that
they would dine there.*

26 When Joseph came home, they brought him the present that they
had carried into the house, and bowed to the ground before him.
[27]*He inquired about their welfare, and said, "Is your father well,
the old man of whom you spoke? Is he still alive?"* [28]*They said,
"Your servant our father is well; he is still alive." And they bowed
their heads and did obeisance.* [29]*Then he looked up and saw his
brother Benjamin, his mother's son, and said, "Is this your youngest
brother, of whom you spoke to me? God be gracious to you, my
son!"* [30]*With that, Joseph hurried out, because he was overcome
with affection for his brother, and he was about to weep. So he went
into a private room and wept there.* [31]*Then he washed his face and
came out; and controlling himself he said, "Serve the meal."* [32]*They
served him by himself, and them by themselves, and the Egyptians
who ate with him by themselves, because the Egyptians could not
eat with the Hebrews, for that is an abomination to the Egyptians.*
[33]*When they were seated before him, the firstborn according to his
birthright and the youngest according to his youth, the men looked
at one another in amazement.* [34]*Portions were taken to them from
Joseph's table, but Benjamin's portion was five times as much as
any of theirs. So they drank and were merry with him.*

Structure

Introductory Notes

In this chapter, which is linked to chapter 44, I have chosen to concentrate on one main component, the greetings. In this chapter we can study in great detail the elevated meaning that greeting has in the community life of the Old Testament. Greetings are not seen here as formal, or even as a polite formality, but rather as an undeniable part of human co-existence, which cannot be rationalized away. A lot can be expressed in a greeting. The storytellers demonstrate this artfulness by the manner in which they use the greetings themselves to develop certain critical stages of the story. This is the same artfulness we have observed so many times before. We can assume that not only is every spoken word of every greeting meant to be taken seriously, but that certain words and gestures are expected in authentic greetings. And in these words and gestures, things can happen that are crucial for the continuation of events.

43:1–14   *The decision to travel*

In the middle of the conversation in which the brothers ask their father to allow Benjamin to accompany them, the father asks: "Why did you treat me so badly as to tell the man that you had another brother?" And the brothers reply, "The man questioned us carefully about ourselves and our kindred, saying, 'Is your father still alive? Have you another brother?'" These are personal, well-meant words of solidarity (compare to 40:7!) But now the brothers are able only to see snares in all such questions – even an innocent question such as this one seems to threaten suspicion and interrogation. One of the most frightening experiences of an encounter with power is that the simple, friendly words of meeting become a weapon turned against the one who has spoken them with friendly and benevolent intent.

Verse 14. "May God Almighty grant you mercy before the man . . ." This parting wish of the father is not a pious phrase. With this wish he sent along something with his sons which was of great importance for the result of the trip. The brothers were compelled to think with fright and perhaps helpless rage of the man who had falsely accused them and thrown them into prison, who still held their brother in chains. With this parting wish the father gives the brothers something to take along which can substantially influence their attitude in the new encounter. In it they learn that even the powerful foreigner is subject to God, and that God is able to make him friendly. We must not thereby forget that in these peoples' thinking, God is the most real of all realities. When the father sends this wish along on his sons' way, they go accompanied by the possibility that God is able to cause the man to release their brother.

43:15–34   *The encounter in Joseph's house*

Verses 16–26. Welcoming is one of the social forms that is most important for contacts among people and their relations with one another. In our text we can expect that every word and gesture at the reception will possess a well-considered meaning which is appropriate to the narrative. First, the contrast must be clarified. In the first reception, the entire action can be characterized by what happens only at the end of the second, namely, that the brothers fall down before the alien lord. The second reception is the conclusion of a long ceremony which, in spite of its menacing nature, presupposes the first. The event has two acts, the first before the steward and the second before Joseph himself. This division presents the difference: the powerful man has a representative, a detail which becomes useful for the story.

For the brothers it is obviously easier to tell the steward what they have on their minds. Therefore the statement of the brothers' intention in vv. 18–23 is contained in the account of their reception by the steward, vv. 17, 24, 25. In the brothers' fear there is the impotent anxiety before the unpredictable menace of the powerful (v. 18), and they bring their protestations of innocence (vv. 19–22) before the deputy. This man, however, takes away their fear. He calms them with the words:

> Rest assured, do not be afraid; your God and the God of your father must have put treasure in your sacks for you; I received your money.

An elegant nuance lies in the fact that this response of the steward's to the brothers' concerned question takes the form of a word of greeting that belongs to their welcome. The greeting has two parts. The *shalom lakaem* is the usual form of greeting for meeting people or receiving guests. It means that the person who arrives is concretely received into the realm of "peace" and security. But also the "do not be afraid" can be a greeting when it is said at a function which frightens the one who receives it. At the same time, the call "do not be afraid" is a promise of salvation which we know best from the proclamation of Deutero-Isaiah and which means to take away the fear from those who are threatened and anxious. As in Deutero-Isaiah it includes a perfective argument which states that something has happened which has eliminated the reason for fear; God has acted (as also in Deutero-Isaiah). The statement, "God has placed a treasure in your grain sacks" is not to be understood, for instance,

in the sense of a fabulous miracle motif. That would not fit
at all into the atmosphere of the Joseph narrative. The
steward knows very well who has put the money into the
sacks, and is not trying to fool the brothers, who also know.
The narrator wishes to say that God, "your God and the
God of your father," was at work in just this way, for his
action in favor of your family is accomplished also by your
having found your money. The brothers do not need to
understand all of this yet. It is enough that the allusion to
the One who acts in all these things comes from the mouth
of this foreigner.

In vv. 24f., the peace with which the steward received
them is made concrete. They can now walk into the coolness
of the house, they can wash their feet and feed their
donkeys. For it is this that is meant here by peace, and with
his words of welcome the steward includes the brothers in
the simple protection of four walls, the possibility to relax
and to rest, to wash themselves and to be restored. And
that the animals receive their feed belongs equally to this
peace, just as in chapter 37:14 Joseph was instructed to
inquire about the *shalom* (welfare) of the flock as well as of
the brothers.

Verses 26–34. In v. 26, there is, in addition to the
prostration before Joseph, the giving of gifts. The simple
act of throwing oneself before another's feet (as at the first
coming of the brothers) denotes subjugation, but when this
action includes the presentation of gifts it signifies a paying
of respects. We are immediately reminded of the wise men
from the East before the manger (Matthew 2:11). We must
be clear about the fact that the brothers come from a famine
and ask for the bread which can save their families from
hunger. Nevertheless, they come bearing a gift for the one
from whom they are asking for bread. In the Old Testament,
the character of a gift is more significant for its social
meaning than for its material reality. It can also mean *beraka*
or "blessing." The presentation of a gift can be a kind of
blessing, and respect and blessing are very closely related.

The greeting of the brothers by Joseph which now follows
belongs to the most beautiful scenes of the entire narrative.
Its theme is *shalom*, and its opens by saying that Joseph
inquired about their welfare. This kind of inquiry is not
something extra added to the greeting, but is in itself a kind

of greeting. By this inquiry, which asks first about the nearest relatives, the one who greets, who has been separated from those who are arriving, includes himself in their circle. This inquiry is a way of establishing contact. In this general motif of greeting the narrator here includes the special burning interest of Joseph for his family: "Is your father well, the old man of whom you spoke? Is he still alive?" This, too, is an inquiry about about *shalom*. Literally, the sentence says, "Does your father have *shalom*?" On the positive answer by the brothers follows the moving question about the youngest brother, whom Joseph visualizes before him, and the special greeting which he sends him, "God be gracious to you, my son!" He uses the same word which we know from the blessing in Numbers 6:25: "the LORD make his face to shine upon you, and be gracious to you." That these words do not appear elsewhere in the Old Testament is an indication that they constitute a special greeting.

The fracture and healing of a society, which is the point of the Joseph narrative, receives a particularly strong and clear expression in this little scene. When at this point Joseph is overpowered by his emotions and must quickly leave the room in order that the brothers may not notice, this emotion points more clearly than could any words to that which is the main point – the wholeness of a society and what that means for those who belong to it.

The common meal which now follows in vv. 32–34 is intimately connected with this point. The meal has an exalted meaning in both the Old Testament and the New Testament. It serves in equal measure and in the same manner both the stilling of hunger and the "building" of a society. The simple satisfaction of hunger would not be considered a meal in the Bible. One need only remember the shared meals of Jesus and his disciples, the last of which demonstrates this in a special way. The meal is not just an expression of a communion (*Gemeinschaft*), but engenders and preserves this commonality. The acceptance of a guest into the fellowship of the meal is therefore simultaneously the granting of participation in one's own existence. Though the description continues to be very lively at this point, it is not necessary to dwell on the details. It is sufficient to call attention once more to the intention of the ending "So they drank and were merry with him." With this is prepared the blunt contrast of these words to the events of the next morning. With this, the narrator calls attention profoundly to the limits of meal fellowship. When the peace of a fellowship has been broken, it cannot be healed by even the happiest camaraderie at table. As the brothers will discover all too soon, harder and more severe events will be necessary for that.

Application

The word "contact" is today a popular word, often with fashionable overtones. We say that a person has difficulty making contacts, we promote evenings which serve to promote human contacts, etc. This chapter has something to say about the meaning of this expression and its use in our society.

Today we hear from all sides and from everyone how important human contacts are for our existence. Because much that is said about this is helpful, especially in contemporary psychology, we ought to concern ourselves with it to a greater extent. Yet this chapter of the Joseph story provides a necessary and helpful correction to that which is generally being said today about difficulties with human contacts and how they may be remedied. We find it strange, at first, that such an astonishing amount of emphasis is laid on that which we call "outer forms" or "forms of social intercourse." That is, on such things as greetings, the polite inquiry, the wish, the gift, and the meal as edification of a fellowship. We have become unfamiliar with the meaning of these processes because of an "ethic of disposition" in which it is continually being said that external forms are not important, but only the intention or the "disposition of the heart." This ethic of dispostion has become mixed with Christian ethics, so that everything is constantly being said to depend, among other things, on Christian or brotherly disposition. In the process, certain important biblical facts come to be ignored and neglected. In our text we notice, at any rate, that surprisingly much is conveyed in the simple processes of human encounter, such as a word of greeting or an inquiry. Or better, astonishingly much can happen because of them. Because of this we must conclude that the forms of encounter which have been given to every human being and to every human society must be taken seriously as possibilities for human contact which determine the nature of our common life. The reason is obvious when we pay attention to the words. The determinitive word is *shalom*, the peace or wholeness of the society, which occurs in the Old Testament in close relation to blessing. Our story deals with the peace and health of society not just in the sense of prayer or forgiveness, but also in the greeting and in the sense of inquiring about others. In other words, the certainty that the peace of a society comes from God, and is based on his blessing, extends into the customary words of greeting and concerned inquiry.

Enlightened by this understanding, we look at our narrative and pose the question about that which happens between people from that instant in which the brothers enter the house of Joseph and until the happy common meal at the end. When we look back at this part of the narrative we will have to consider in particular that at its center stands the cry, "Do not be afraid!" with which a stranger with an alien faith reminded the brothers of their God and of the God of their fathers.

8

The Silver Cup (Genesis 44)

Text

44 Then he commanded the steward of his house, "Fill the men's sacks with food, as much as they can carry, and put each man's money in the top of his sack. ²Put my cup, the silver cup, in the top of the sack of the youngest, with his money for the grain." And he did as Joseph told him. ³As soon as the morning was light, the men were sent away with their donkeys. ⁴When they had gone only a short distance from the city, Joseph said to his steward. "Go, follow after the men; and when you overtake them, say to them, 'Why have you returned evil for good? Why have you stolen my silver cup? ⁵Is it not from this that my lord drinks? Does he not indeed use it for divination? You have done wrong in doing this.'"

6 When he overtook them, he repeated these words to them. ⁷They said to him, "Why does my lord speak such words as these? Far be it from your servants that they should do such a thing! ⁸Look, the money that we found at the top of our sacks, we brought back to you from the land of Canaan; why then would we steal silver or gold from your lord's house? ⁹Should it be found with any one of your servants, let him die; moreover the rest of us will become my lord's slaves." ¹⁰He said, "Even so; in accordance with your words, let it be: he with whom it is found shall become my slave, but the rest of you shall go free." ¹¹Then each one quickly lowered his sack to the ground, and each opened his sack. ¹²He searched, beginning with the eldest and ending with the youngest; and the cup was found in Benjamin's sack. ¹³At this they tore their clothes. Then each one loaded his donkey, and they returned to the city.

14 Judah and his brothers came to Joseph's house while he was still there; and they fell to the ground before him. ¹⁵Joseph said to them, "What deed is this that you have done? Do you not know that one such as I can practice divination?" ¹⁶And Judah said, "What can we say to my lord? What can we speak? How can we clear ourselves? God has found out the guilt of your servants; here we are then, my

lord's slaves, both we and also the one in whose possession the cup has been found." [17]*But he said, "Far be it from me that I should do so! Only the one in whose possession the cup was found shall be my slave; but as for you, go up in peace to your father."*

18 *Then Judah stepped up to him and said, "O my lord, let your servant please speak a word in my lord's ears, and do not be angry with your servant; for you are like Pharaoh himself.* [19]*My lord asked his servants, saying, 'Have you a father or a brother?'* [20]*And we said to my lord, 'We have a father, an old man, and a young brother, the child of his old age. His brother is dead; he alone is left of his mother's children, and his father loves him.'* [21]*Then you said to your servants, 'Bring him down to me, so that I may set my eyes on him.'* [22]*We said to my lord, 'The boy cannot leave his father, for if he should leave his father, his father would die.'* [23]*Then you said to your servants. 'Unless your youngest brother comes down with you, you shall see my face no more.'* [24]*When we went back to your servant my father we told him the words of my lord.* [25]*And when our father said, 'Go again, buy us a little food,'* [26]*we said, 'We cannot go down. Only if our youngest brother goes with us, will we go down; for we cannot see the man's face unless our youngest brother is with us.'* [27]*Then your servant my father said to us, 'You know that my wife bore me two sons;* [28]*one left me, and I said, Surely he has been torn to pieces; and I have never seen him since.* [29]*If you take this one also from me, and harm comes to him, you will bring down my gray hairs in sorrow to Sheol.'* [30]*Now therefore, when I come to your servant my father and the boy is not with us, then, as his life is bound up in the boy's life,* [31]*when he sees that the boy is not with us, he will die; and your servants will bring down the gray hairs of your servant our father with sorrow to Sheol.* [32]*For your servant became surety for the boy to my father, saying, 'If I do not bring him back to you, then I will bear the blame in the sight of my father all my life.'* [33]*Now therefore, please let your servant remain as a slave to my lord in place of the boy; and let the boy go back with his brothers.* [34]*For how can I go back to my father if the boy is not with me? I fear to see the suffering that would come upon my father."*

Structure

1–17		Answering for the guilt
	1–2	The contrived crime
	3–6	The (false) accusation
	7–9	Rejection of the guilt and defense

Interpretation

The structure of the story is a judicial proceeding. A theft has seemingly occurred and been discovered, and the matter is being considered. Judicial or court proceedings furnish the outline for many narratives in the Old Testament, stories as diverse as Genesis 3 and 2 Samuel 12. In such cases it is assumed that the legal proceedings are very much closer to daily living than they seem in our day. In the small local Israelite settlements judicial proceedings constituted one of the most important ingredients of public life. That has been beautifully demonstrated by L. Köhler in "*Die Hebräische Rechtsgemeinde*". It seems to be the case that in very recent times there is once more a stronger feeling that judicial proceedings belong to the center of human existence. That can be seen, for instance, in F. Kafka's *The Trial*, in which the structure of the entire work is also a judicial process. In our interpretation of chapter 44, therefore, we can assume that the point of this process is not crime as a special topic but rather the decisive proceedings of the human condition in general.

44:1–17 *Answering for the guilt*

Verse 1–2. Here a crime is concocted, and a trap is laid for innocent people into which they will inevitably have to fall. Any moral condemnation of this attitude of Joseph should be rejected from the outset. The intention of the narrator is that the brothers be brought to a situation which is exceptionally analagous to that which had been the root of the entire action. It cannot even be said that he wishes to test the brothers. And yet with the repetition of the original situation a question is placed before the brothers. How will they react?

Verses 3–6. On their way home, the brothers are overtaken by the unjustified accusation of having committed a crime of which they were innocent. Central to the accusation is the question: "Why have you returned evil for good?" After they had breathed easier with the friendly reception and the fulfillment of their anxious requests, this was a surprise which once more pulled all solid ground out from under their feet. Once more they are defenseless in the hands of the mighty man.

Verses 7–9. Because they are conscious of their innocence, the brothers pronounce the death sentence over the guilty one who could not be among them: "Should it be found with any of your servants, let him die . . ." As the story progresses, however, this indignant insistence on their innocence only tends to exacerbate their powerlessness. The next verses demonstrate this.

Verses 10–12. The tension of this moment is presented in the story with simplicity and power. After only a few sentences the result appears, "and the cup was found in Benjamin's sack." Now it sounds like derision when the punishment which the brothers have specified is softened by the steward, "he with whom it is found shall become my slave." (The steward speaks in Joseph's name.)

Verses 13–14. In place of speaking of the brothers' feelings at this point, the storyteller's art inserts a short silence in the events. In a few words the return to the city is told. At the same time, however, these verses set the stage for what comes next. The return from the place at which the bogus crime was discovered to the person who must pronounce the sentence points silently to that which will then follow, which is a turning back in another sense.

That this is really meant can be seen from the tension between the speech of the brothers after the first accusation and their speech after the repetition of the accusation in v. 15. Verses 13–14 represent, in the first place, a turning back to a higher authority; from the police who caught the thief to the judge who must pronounce the sentence. But in the background there is also the portrayal of an appeal to a superior court. Before this higher instance the offense – which they have not committed – is seen in a wider perspective.

Verse 15. Once more the brothers stand before Joseph. He repeats the accusation. Once more his words must have sounded to them like terrible derision: "Do you not know that such a man as I can indeed divine?" Once more the statement is murky, understandable only in the light of what follows.

Verse 16. The contrast between the confession of guilt which follows here and vv. 7–9 is astonishing. Not even a remnant remains of the earlier indignant rejection of guilt. The return to the city separates the two (vv. 13–14). It is not necessary to explain why Judah now speaks so differently. All is said with the decisive statement, "God has found out the guilt of your servants."

What is the meaning of this confession of guilt?

The eldest brother, as the one responsible, has put this situation, which at the moment seems incomprehensible and meaningless (contrast with the happy meal on the night before!) into context, and has so given it meaning. God has revealed what the brothers had sought to conceal. Therefore, though he is innocent, he declares himself to be guilty. Now it is suddenly no longer decisive that the brothers are innocent in this matter. What is decisive is that the blow which struck them gains its meaning from their buried guilt. Here it is perceived that guilt, punishment and forgiveness have their authentic reality only in relation with the real history of a person and a people, not in religious abstraction or cultic scheme. It is recognized that in the hidden relation of guilt, punishment and forgiveness there is a power of historical binding. The life of the brothers becomes a totality which stretches from that deed to this discovery, and so gains significance. It no longer consists in unrelated individual acts which have been forgotten or will be forgotten, but rather in the discovery which illuminates their existence as a way watched over by God.

This acknowledgment of the relatedness of all things is made concrete by the oldest brother when he stands up to confess the collective guilt. Thus the confession of guilt becomes an act of human freedom in responsibility. Precisely in this is freedom revealed, that in a situation in which he has no guilt, he confesses.

Verse 17. The recognition of the guilt which has now been revealed should show itself in a readiness to accept the punishment, even though at that moment it would be innocently-suffered punishment. But just at this point there appears the complication which makes everything more difficult; the punishment is declared to be for the youngest brother alone. Thus, the reconstitution of the original situation has been attained; now everything is just as it once was. The one difference is that now the brothers do not need to lie to their father, for they have faced superior authority against which they have been helpless. With this, the brothers are encountering a decision which involves more than just the present hour. It is a decision which takes into account the newly-discovered totality, a decision which needs to take into account the consequences of the error which had now been revealed.

44:18–34   *Standing up for the brother*
The solemn and ceremonious nature of Judah's request to speak lends importance to the speech which it introduces. Something decisive is being said here. Judah asks to speak because he is the one who is responsible. Because it is he who will be questioned by the father and will have to answer him, he is the spokesman for the brothers at the turning point of the action. Because he will later have to speak, he is now empowered to speak. Speech and responsibility are closely associated. The accountability of the oldest brother reveals itself here even in its most extreme implications.

Verses 19–34. Like the discourse of a messenger, Judah's speech has an indicative part as well as an imperative part that is grounded in the indicative. The whole account of that which had previously happened (vv. 19–34) serves only to explain and to furnish a basis for the real request which

Judah makes of Joseph (v. 33). (The following verse, v. 34, gives one more brief summary of the explanation.) The indicative portion is so organized that vv. 19–29 speak of what has already happened, while vv. 30–31 speak of what will happen when the brothers return home without the youngest brother. In this so conspicuous and clearly organized discourse by Judah, the narrator comes to the goal of the inner motif of his narrative. While the external action does not reach its conclusion until later, that which happens among the father, brothers, and youngest brother reaches its conclusion in these words of Judah.

Verses 19–29. Judah's detailed account of what has happened until then has, in the first place, the function of supporting his plea to Joseph. In the narrative as a whole, it has a meaning which goes beyond this; it presents that which has happened as a totality which includes the first act, the loss of Joseph. Thereby is confirmed the interpretation we have given to the confession of guilt. Even though Judah does not say anything in his report about the crime of the brothers – when he explains that the father has already once lost his youngest son, and that if he were to lose the one who is now the youngest, it would mean his death – he brings together that which happened earlier with that which has just occurred. The decisive point is that the eldest brother now sees eye to eye with his father about what has happened.

Verses 30–31. On the basis of his account he can now explain what will happen when the brothers come home without the one with whom the father's life "is bound up." It is in these words that the connection to the beginning and thereby also to the unified vision of the past and present are most clearly expressed. Earlier they had managed to listen to their father's bitter lament (37:33f.) without reacting. Now Judah says, "when he sees that the boy is not with us, he will die; and your servants will bring down the gray hairs of your servant our father with sorrow to Sheol." These are the same words that had earlier been spoken by Jacob! And in this sentence Judah assumes with his brothers the responsibility, "your servants . . . to Sheol." With his words, Judah clearly indicates that something has changed.

Verses 32–34. What Judah said previously was said in the capacity of responsible spokesman for all the brothers.

Now, however, he steps out of the fraternal circle and speaks for himself alone. Judah does not beg the Egyptian lord for grace; he accepts the guilt and thereby also its punishment. His plea has to do only with the concern that the punishment is falling on the wrong person, and he wishes to take it upon himself. Thus the narrator calls attention to an entirely new possibility for life in fellowship. What Judah is offering is something unprecedented for ancient thought. In two respects it is discontinuous with tradition: first, it would break the link between an action and its consequence, second, it would transform the meaning of punishment, previously seen as something absolutely negative. The punishment assumed in this way serves the healing of society. We do not know how far the narrator carried out this thought, nor whether he assigned to it any more general validity. We must take care not to introduce something into the text here. One thing, however, emerges clearly from the direction of the story: the narrator means to say here that an individual's intercession on behalf of others can, in certain circumstances, contribute to the healing of a society. Here, for the first time in the Bible, we hear of the possibility of a substitutionary action which serves the common good.

The last verse is a beautiful expression of the Joseph story's openness to the limits and possibilities of the human condition: "I fear to see the suffering that would come upon my father."

Application

In teaching this chapter it is important to make plain that here the narrator has stated what is important to him. It represents not just the turning point but also the internal high point of the narrative. The chapter is also so rich in relationships to our own contemporary existence that one must guard against many (unwarranted) digressions and applications. Everything here depends in a very special way simply on our willingness to allow these events to speak for themselves. For this reason we must certainly present the text in a way that is consistent with its structure.

We can begin with the assumption that we have become so accustomed in our churchly use of language to speak about sin, punishment, and forgiveness in such a generalized and abstract manner that these concepts have largely lost their power and vitality. This narrative is not based on the concept of sin and forgiveness, but on their reality in human existence. Sin and forgiveness do not normally exist in a direct and obvious relation to one another. After the brothers' crime nothing happened for many years. Everything stayed as it was, and somehow everything was set right again. For years it was possible for the brothers to believe that they had succeeded in concealing their guilt. Life went on. But then came the day when God disclosed their guilt, and in an entirely different context! With this the Bible tells us that we human beings need forgiveness, that we we cannot manage without it, and that we are not able really to hide our guilt. God lays it bare so that society can once more be healed. That, however, does not happen schematically and visibly, so that God punishes the guilty, or so that an offense is followed directly by penitence and forgiveness. In real life it just does not happen that way. What is astonishing and profound is that God continues to work in those who have not confessed their guilt but persist in hiding it. He does not give up on them. And he can guide things so that such a person is led to admit his guilt at an entirely different place and in an entirely different situation. Just in this way God can heal a broken fellowship where, judging by human opinion, there is nothing but hopeless obduracy. In just the same way, however, meaning and coherence can enter a life through the acceptance and confession of long-past guilt. The theologian who narrates this wishes through this story to tell us about the activity of the God who desires peace among men and creates it in a way that is often hidden to us. At the same time, he wants to tell us that we need to take seriously the full humanity of humankind wherever we see this God at work.

9

Joseph Reveals Himself and Offers Forgiveness (Genesis 45)

Text

45 *Then Joseph could no longer control himself before all those who stood by him, and he cried out, "Send everyone away from me." So no one stayed with him when Joseph made himself known to his brothers.* *²And he wept so loudly that the Egyptians heard it, and the household of Pharaoh heard it. ³Joseph said to his brothers, "I am Joseph. Is my father still alive?" But his brothers could not answer him, so dismayed were they at his presence.*

4 Then Joseph said to his brothers, "Come closer to me." And they came closer. He said, "I am your brother, Joseph, whom you sold into Egypt. ⁵And now do not be distressed, or angry with yourselves, because you sold me here; for God sent me before you to preserve life. ⁶For the famine has been in the land these two years; and there are five more years in which there will be neither plowing nor harvest. ⁷God sent me before you to preserve for you a remnant on earth, and to keep alive for you many survivors. ⁸So it was not you who sent me here, but God; he has made me a father to Pharaoh, and lord of all his house and ruler over all the land of Egypt. ⁹Hurry and go up to my father and say to him, "Thus says your son Joseph, God has made me lord of all Egypt; come down to me, do not delay. ¹⁰You shall settle in the land of Goshen, and you shall be near me, you and your children and your children's children, as well as your flocks, your herds, and all that you have. ¹¹I will provide for you there – since there are five more years of famine to come – so that you and your household, and all that you have, will not come to poverty.' ¹²And now your eyes and the eyes of my brother Benjamin see that it is my own mouth that speaks to you. ¹³You must tell my father how greatly I am honored in Egypt, and all that you have seen. Hurry and bring my father down here." ¹⁴Then he fell upon his brother Benjamin's neck and wept, while Benjamin wept upon his neck. ¹⁵And he

93

kissed all his brothers and wept upon them; and after that his brothers talked with him.

16 When the report was heard in Pharaoh's house, "Joseph's brothers have come," Pharaoh and his servants were pleased. ¹⁷*Pharaoh said to Joseph, "Say to your brothers, 'Do this: load your animals and go back to the land of Canaan. ¹⁸Take your father and your households and come to me, so that I may give you the best of the land of Egypt, and you may enjoy the fat of the land.' ¹⁹You are further charged to say, 'Do this: take wagons from the land of Egypt for your little ones and for your wives, and bring your father, and come. ²⁰Give no thought to your possessions, for the best of all the land of Egypt is yours.'"*

21 The sons of Israel did so. Joseph gave them wagons according to the instruction of Pharaoh, and he gave them provisions for the journey. ²²*To each one of them he gave a set of garments; but to Benjamin he gave three hundred pieces of silver and five sets of garments. ²³To his father he sent the following: ten donkeys loaded with the good things of Egypt, and ten female donkeys loaded with grain, bread, and provision for his father on the journey. ²⁴Then he sent his brothers on their way, and as they were leaving he said to them, "Do not quarrel along the way."*

25 So they went up out of Egypt and came to their father Jacob in the land of Canaan. ²⁶*And they told him, "Joseph is still alive! He is even ruler over all the land of Egypt." He was stunned; he could not believe them. ²⁷But when they told him all the words of Joseph that he had said to them, and when he saw the wagons that Joseph had sent to carry him, the spirit of their father Jacob revived. ²⁸Israel said, "Enough! My son Joseph is still alive. I must go and see him before I die."*

Structure

Interpretation

It is conspicuous that Judah apparently receives no answer at all to the words he has addressed to the Egyptian minister and which are accorded such great importance in the narrative. By requesting that all the Egyptians around him leave, Joseph alters the scene. That which now happens is within the circle of the brothers. With this, however, the addressee to whom Judah directed his words has now become a different person. The words of Judah have revealed to his brother that a transformation has taken place in the brothers. When he now reveals himself to them as their brother, the exterior transformation thereby completes the one that took place on the interior. Now forgiveness and reconciliation have become possible. Judah's words were therefore by no means in vain; they receive their answer, even though it is a totally unexpected one.

Joseph's revelation of who he is inevitably comes as a terrible fright to the brothers (v. 3b). For this reason he frames his next statement in order to assuage their fear and their confusion (v. 5a) by lending his brothers' offense ("because you sold me here") a new meaning (v. 7). From the context it becomes clear that with the statement, "God sent me before you . . .", Joseph is expressing to the brothers his forgiveness. He hides the direct statement of forgiveness behind this sentence, in which he removes the weight of guilt from them: "You do not need to be anxious any longer, for everything has turned out well." Judah had offered to atone for the wrong through his readiness to take upon himself the punishment. In place of this atonement, Joseph's redeeming word offers the forgiveness that makes such an atonement unnecessary because it brings about a healing that brings everyone back together again. In this presentation the emphasis is on the healing through

forgiveness. This healing, moreover, is further exalted by
the fact that the reunification of the family now results in
both its preservation and its protection: "to preserve for you
a remnant on earth."

All the weight is placed on the words which compare
the deeds of the brothers to the actions of God. This is
clearest when the narrator explains and expands the
statement, "So it was not you who sent me here, but God."

The same statement appears three times in this speech.
It is plain how the narrator dwells on it and underlines it,
as if he wants to say to his hearers that here they can find
what this story is all about. It is about God's rule over human
activity, God's guidance of destinies which can totally
transform human plans and make out of them something
which corresponds to God's plan (50:20). This divine rule,
however, desires the life of human beings. That which God
has created God also desires to preserve. For this reason
there appears in this part of Joseph's speech, which contrasts
the brothers' evil deed with his benevolent response, a
completely different contrast; the one between the seven
years of famine, which menace the lives of many people
and families, and the wonderful deliverance that God's
providence set into action long before, thus preserving the
lives of many. These words are permeated by praise for the
God who preserves and upholds life, just as we hear in the
Psalms. This praise of the God who protects is bound up
with the perception, developed in the story, that the
preserving acts of God can be profoundly obscured behind
a foreground of human activity that is marked by life-
denying forces, hatred, and lies. When the hour arrives,
however, the superficial surface of this foreground activity
is torn away, and the human being is enabled to perceive
behind it the life-defending activity of God and to
understand: ". . . it was not you who sent me here, but God."

In the work already mentioned above, von Rad says
about this point, "Here Joseph finally speaks openly of God,
and here the last veil is lifted, for here appears openly that
which is in reality the principal theme of the entire story:
the hand of God, which desires to lead to a gracious end all
the confusions of human guilt. Joseph wishes to concentrate
all attention on that which is most important: the leading
of God, which had made use of all of these dark things for

good" (pp. 191f.). A little later, von Rad continues, "I do not wish to conceal the fact that this extremely comforting word of Joseph, because of its plainly abrupt separation of divine and human activity, stands at the beginning of a way which is theologically questionable. For it relegates God's activity to a radical hiddenness, distance and imperceptibility." Citing Ecclesiastes 3:11; 8:17; 11:5 he says: "The preacher's scepticism has roots which go back very far!" (pp. 22f.)

This reference to the limit of what is said in Joseph's talk must be taken very seriously. It is based on the fact that von Rad views the Joseph story as closely related to wisdom; in relation to 50:20 he calls attention especially to the words:

The human mind plans the way, but the LORD directs the steps. (Proverbs 16:9)

All our steps are ordered by the LORD; how then can we understand our own ways? (Proverbs 20:24)

Although the content of these words is very close to the sum of the Joseph narrative, one must not overlook the fact that the words of Joseph in 45:4–8 are spoken at a moment in which, as von Rad himself says, "the veil is lifted," that is, in which the wonderful life-preserving activity becomes *evident*! All of the pathos of our text lies precisely in this, that the veil was lifted and that *knowledge* became possible. The hiddenness of God's action is not being examined here *per se*, but rather in relation to its objective, and the objective is the preservation and protection of life. Therefore I see these words in greater proximity to the praise of God which we know from the Psalms, the praise of the God who preserves and protects. This vision does not become dangerous until God's hidden activity is abstracted from its goal, the preservation and protection of life, and is viewed for itself and in absolute terms.

Verses 25–28. It will be necessary only to say a few words about the conclusion of the chapter. What is important here is the effect on Jacob of the returning brothers' message, "He was stunned; he could not believe them." How much a simple sentence like this one can say! It is one of the many sentences in the Joseph narrative which have the power to bridge over great expanses of time. Here we hear that the lie with which the brothers concealed their guilt had, after all, had a further effect. It now becomes clear that the father has become distrustful. When the peace and integrity of a community is broken at one point, it has its effect on everything. When suspicion prevails it remains and destroys everything. So it becomes clear once again in these final words how profound the rent was and how wonderful its healing.

That which the healing of the community means for the father is also said in a highly simple but succinct manner "Jacob revived" and exclaimed "Enough! My son Joseph is still alive; I must go and see him before I die." With this – so the narrator wishes to say – the father's lament from the beginning (37:34f.) is stilled. His approach to death is transformed. Now he will not be brought down "with sorrow to Sheol," but he will see his child and thereby experience the integrity of his life cycle, so that he can die in peace.

The account of the whole story ends, therefore, with the statement that an old man is able to die in peace. In this concluding statement the magnificent and profound humanity of the story is revealed once again.

Application

Because chapter 45 constitutes both the high point and the real conclusion of the Joseph story – nothing essentially new follows it – much of the presentation of the text will depend on the previous formulation of the series, and can for this reason vary widely. If one considers only this chapter, the presentation can be divided according to the three groups of texts that were emphasized in the interpretation.

In the first part we tell how the forgiving word of Joseph produces the solution for obduracy, the solution for all confusion, the solution for fear. Above all it will be important to show how, in a word of human forgiveness, something of the thoughts of peace which God has toward our human world (Jeremiah 29) can be realized. Our story gives us the possibility of transmitting to modern hearers something of the meaning-giving power which can radiate from a word of forgiveness. However, our story also shows that it must be spoken at the right place and at the right time. Obviously it would not have been appropriate at the happy meeting on the previous evening. It must remain a uniquely precious word.

In the second part, the interpretation of the action is to be developed from 50:20. Enough has already been said about it in this interpretation and earlier in the introduction. It remains for the presenter to decide between the two directions of interpretation alluded to above, that is, whether he wants to interpret the text more in terms of wisdom (von Rad) or more in terms of the praise of God.

In the third part, the presentation as well as the narrative itself will return to the simple lines of the suffering and the joy of the father. From the words of the text one can look over into our reality. That an old man dies in peace is the goal of the entire story. How greatly the welfare of a society even today depends on this, that this "death in peace" is taken seriously, that the peace of God is taken seriously as something that extends even to the death of an aged person!

We end our hearing of the story of Joseph by meditating on the relation between this peaceful death and the liberating affirmation of our guilt and of the saving and forgiving word.

10

Jacob Blesses the Pharaoh
(Genesis 47: 7–10)

The concluding part, chapters 46–50 (without 49) can be described in widely differing ways. In addition to concluding what had previously been related – that is, Jacob's journey to Egypt, the reunion with his son Joseph, the settlement in Egypt, the death and burial of the father, and finally, Joseph's death after he has once more forgiven the brothers – chapters 46–50 include various elaborations which are dispensable to any presentation of the entire story of Joseph. Out of the entire concluding section we will deal with only one more scene: how Jacob was introduced to the Pharaoh by his son and how he blesses him. This scene belongs to the priestly document (P), to which belong in chapters 37–50, beyond the first words in chapter 37 and several fragments, only a few short passages in chapters 47–50.

Text

⁷Then Joseph brought in his father Jacob, and presented him before Pharaoh, and Jacob blessed Pharaoh. ⁸Pharaoh said to Jacob, "How many are the years of your life?" ⁹Jacob said to Pharaoh, "The years of my earthly sojourn are one hundred thirty; few and hard have been the years of my life. They do not compare with the years of the life of my ancestors during their long sojourn." ¹⁰Then Jacob blessed Pharaoh, and went out from the presence of Pharaoh.

Interpretation

It is not difficult to imagine this scene in which the old man

is led before the throne of Pharaoh, into what for him were
alien, oppressive, and luxurious surroundings, into a circle
of the king's ministers and officials, each of whom must
have looked to Jacob like the exalted official had looked to
his sons when they came asking for grain. Nevertheless,
Jacob's appearance in this short scene reveals a special
dignity. Jacob is led before Pharaoh, and he blesses him. An
old foreigner, a shepherd from the steppe who, through his
sons, had to ask Pharaoh's minister for bread, performs the
gesture of blessing on the powerful and divine one!

The question of what the editor of the priestly document
wanted to say with this scene, and what he wanted to say
with it at this juncture, is more difficult to answer. Because
P does not have a developed Joseph narrative, the scene
actually belongs according to its structure to the cycle of
the Jacob narratives and is placed shortly before their
conclusion and at the transition from the history of the
patriarchs to the events of the Exodus which began in Egypt.
It is in this transition that the scene receives its special
meaning. Blessing is a concept that in the time of the
patriarchs was definitive for the action of God. But P knows
also a blessing which is meant for the Creation (Genesis
1:28); the blessing of man is bound up with his creation. At
the end of the history of the patriarchs in P there is the
blessing of Pharaoh by Jacob as a sign that the blessing
bestowed on the patriarchs and passed along from the
fathers to the children (as when in chapter 48 Jacob blesses
Ephraim and Manasseh) reaches beyond the succession of
the patriarchs and is a blessing intended for humanity.
Moreover, the scene reveals the relation of the priestly
blessing which was established in the course of the giving
of the Law (Numbers 6:24–46) with the blessing of the
patriarchs from which it derives.

The conversation between the two men seems to have
been conventional and without content, as tends to be the
case at audiences and receptions. But we have found
repeatedly that in the history of the patriarchs such forms
of encounter are taken very seriously, and that every word
in them has its meaning and its function. Pharaoh asks about
Jacob's age. For an instant, the question unites the person
who has the office of king with the humble stranger. It asks
about that which is common to both of them: the way which

leads from childhood to the prime years of a man's life to old age and the approach of death. Jacob understands the question in this way. He takes it seriously and responds to the interest with a partial answer. His 130 years were for Jacob "few and hard," the number of years stands in place of a history. Both the words, however, with which he characterizes this history contain a contradiction or even an offense.

Jacob calls 130 years a short life. Although his fathers had become still older, and advanced age was considered a sign of a special favor from God, Jacob knew that a great many people in his surroundings had attained only a fragment of this length, and that popular opinion considered it a long life. When he calls his life short, this is the expression of a perception of human life that has learned to see into remote periods of time. Perhaps he also said something else to the Pharaoh which the latter understood in relation to his fathers' pyramids and to his own.

When Jacob says of his life that it was "hard," this is also not simply an insightful description of his existence. Jacob stands before Pharaoh as the one who had been saved with his family from famine, the one who had been reunited with his son, the one protected in the midst of many threats. In the sense of the P document, one can understand what he says here of his life only in terms of the blessing which determines the entire scene. Jacob says this as the blessed one who is able to bless. And so he says that his life as one blessed has been one full of suffering. Just this has been the mature fruit of his experience with God. He had learned that the blessed one continues to be a person with limitations and failures. He has experienced that God's blessing can be bound up with his "strange act," with the misery of the refugee, with the helplessness of the servant, with the bowing down before the unblessed brother. He has been blessed with many sons, but the blessing has brought him bitter suffering. These experiences formed the answer that Jacob gives Pharaoh here.

Nothing more happens except that Jacob blesses Pharaoh before taking his leave from him. And this, too, is more than just a form. That which is meant by blessing in the Old Testament can be illustrated especially by a passage in the book of Job, where Job, in retrospect over his previous

existence, says "The blessing of the wretched came upon
me . . ." (29:13; see 31:20). Though blessing here includes
giving thanks, it is nevertheless much more than this. Even
a beggar can bless a rich and powerful person. The poorest
and most miserable has in blessing something which he
can give. For in blessing God is at work, and the one who
blesses transmits in his blessing the blessing of God. Human
dignity is grounded in this, that every person has this
possibility of blessing another, that is, to bring him or her
into touch with the power of God through his word of
blessing. Not even the most miserable person loses this
possibility. It is not only the priest and the king who can
bless; also the beggar and the lost. When the dying father
blesses his children, it is thereby said that this existence
which now goes to its end possessed the possibility and
capability of blessing, and that in this was his dignity.

This casts a light on the characteristic fact that in Hebrew
the word which means "to bless," *barak*, can also mean to
laud or to praise. The Old Testament sees in the praise of
God precisely the existence which is fulfilled and real: "The
living, the living, they thank you, as I do today" (Isaiah
38:19). Praise of God and blessing belong together in the
sense that in both a person binds himself and his fellow
men with the stream of power that sets in motion all that
takes place with the "spring of life." The dignity of human
beings is based on the possibility of this bond. The
possibility of praising God and of blessing a fellow human
being sticks with a person in all exaltation and in all the
abysses of his existence. It persists for him and belongs to
his human nature because God has created him in God's
image. The fact that God created human beings according
to his own image is the foundation of their dignity. The
image of God in human beings does not consist, for instance,
in anything which can be verified about man; rather, God
made human beings like himself and thereby gave them
the possibility of this bond.

With this blessing, peace is intimately connected. The
Joseph story tells of the breaking of peace and of its healing.
The peace of a society lives off of God's power to bless.
When this peace breaks down, healing is only possible
through the rediscovery of the link to this power (44:16). In
the blessing of Pharaoh by Jacob here at the conclusion of

the Joseph story, this bond of peace with blessing is once more emphasized. It lies on the path on to which Abraham was sent by God with the promise that, "in you shall all the families of the earth be blessed" (12:1–3). And thereby this blessing of the Pharaoh by Jacob points beyond itself to a story whose purpose is the definitive conclusion of the peace which avails for all people.

Application

Because this Bible study is to be the conclusion of the entire series, the most important motifs and directions should be heard one more time and be placed in a larger context.

As a point of departure one can begin with the question of human dignity in our times. What do we understand by this today? Where and how does it appear in a special way in our day? How and in what way is it being especially threatened in this epoch of the masses and of machines? And we ask further what the Bible says about human dignity, what is to be understood by this, and what this can mean for our times. This approach brings us to the scene in which Jacob is presented to the Pharaoh and blesses him. That which we mean by human worth is expressed here in a strong and characteristic manner. The scene radiates something of the human values that make it clear that despite the great distance between the king of the Egyptian empire and the humble wandering shepherd, Jacob represents something, and has something to say which will reach up to Pharaoh's level. What is it?

This scene, with the words that are exchanged in it, is to be presented in such a way as to speak for itself. At the end the question will remain: What is the meaning of Jacob's blessing of the Pharaoh, and what really happens in the blessing?

Now it is necessary to explain in a few essential movements, following perhaps the interpretation which has been given, what blessing means in the Old Testament. In relation to the affinity between blessing and peace we can once more review the principal parts of the Joseph story, which in turn is finally to be placed into the broader context of the entire patriarchal history by means of the arc that stretches from the promise to Abraham in Genesis 12:1–3 to this blessing of the Pharaoh by the aged Jacob. It is then also possible to see the even broader connection, the place of the Joseph narrative in the whole Bible, as well as to call attention to the goal toward which the Joseph story, as a part of the history of the patriarchs, is moving.

11

Ultimate Forgiveness (Genesis 50:15–21)

Text

15 Realizing that their father was dead, Joseph's brothers said, "What if Joseph still bears a grudge against us and pays us back in full for all the wrong that we did to him?" 16So they approached Joseph, saying, "Your father gave this instruction before he died, 17'Say to Joseph: I beg you, forgive the crime of your brothers and the wrong they did in harming you.' Now therefore please forgive the crime of the servants of the God of your father." Joseph wept when they spoke to him. 18Then his brothers also wept, fell down before him, and said, "We are here as your slaves." 19But Joseph said to them, "Do not be afraid! Am I in the place of God? 20Even though you intended to do harm to me, God intended it for good, in order to preserve a numerous people, as he is doing today. 21So have no fear; I myself will provide for you and your little ones." In this way he reassured them, speaking kindly to them.

Structure

15–21	The true conclusion of the Joseph narrative
15	The brothers' fear after the father's death
16–17	Message to Joseph based on the father and his deeds
18	The brothers' offer to become Joseph's slaves
19–21	Joseph's reply: pardon and provision
19	Do not be afraid; am I in the place of God?
20	You – but God
21	So have no fear; I myself will provide for you.

This outline is based on the sum of the promises of salvation, especially as they occur in the proclamation of Deutero-Isaiah; following on the account of the brothers' fear, which was revived at the moment when the father is no longer alive (v. 15), and of their attempt to escape the threatening wrath or ire of Joseph by appealing to their fathers' memory (vv. 16f.), comes the meeting. The brothers in their fear are content to become Joseph's slaves, and fall down before him with this offer. This is once more the dream motif, heightened by the offer of the voluntary servitude. Into this situation comes the answer of Joseph, which takes away all their fear and assures them of full forgiveness. Joseph's response begins with the "do not be afraid" of the assurance of salvation. Here, as in Deutero-Isaiah, his answer is based on the present (here only a question expecting a negative answer: "Am I ..."), on the past (what God has done, which receives most attention), and on the future ("I myself will provide for you ..."). Thus, with the pledge for the future in mind, the theme "Do not fear" is reiterated. This total agreement of Joseph's response with the assurance of salvation is astonishing. But what does it imply for our understanding of its central statement? The statement says:

> Even though you intended to do harm to me, God intended it for good, in order to preserve a numerous people, as he is doing today." (v. 20)

Viewed under the aspect of the structure of the salvation statement, this sentence represents an expansion, and its core is an affirmation based on God's acts in the past. God intended it for good. Everything else explains and broadens this decisive statement. The statement is meant to take away the brothers' fear. It is therefore no generalized *assertion* about God – in which respect it differs essentially from the proverbial statements which von Rad cites on this point (see the material on chapter 45) – but rather *encouragement* which proclaims what God has done. One can find in this sentence an almost classical explanation of *providentia Dei*, God's providence. And yet we must at the same time understand that this is not a doctrine about divine providence, but a witness to a specific act of God, experienced in a concrete situation, which does not, however, refer to the actions of God in a general sense at all, but rather to a very specific life–preserving action. It is this to which Joseph witnesses here, and in this he praises God, who in the midst of the evil action of the brothers and of Joseph's suffering, secretly blesses and preserves. Joseph's comforting words to his brothers are therefore in essence praise of God. For a further interpretation I refer to the commentary on chapter 45 and to what was said in the Introduction.

At the conclusion of the entire series, one can review the course of the whole narrative from the viewpoint of the Introduction. There is probably no other part of the Bible which speaks of God in such human terms. In this way we are led to ask if all our statements about God are not far too burdened by thoughts and ideas which are entirely untouched by the Bible's unique message about God.

Recommended Reading

Commentaries

Brueggemann, Walter. *Genesis*, Interpretation. Philadelphia: Westminster Press, 1986.
Simpson, C. A. *Genesis*, Interpreter's Bible. New York and Nashville: 1952.
Skinner, John. *Genesis*, International Critical Commentary. Edinburgh: T&T Clark, 1930, 1994.
Von Rad, Gerhard. *Genesis: A Commentary*. Philadelphia: Westminster Press, 1973; London: SCM Press, 1979.
Westermann, Claus. *Genesis 37–50*. Minneapolis: Fortress Press, 1986; London: SPCK, 1987.
Westermann, Claus. *Genesis*. Edinburgh, T&T Clark, 1988.

Other works

Argyle, A. W. "Joseph the Patriarch in Patristic Teaching," *Expository Times* 67 (1956), pp. 199–201.
Dresner, Samuel H. *Rachel*. Minneapolis: Fortress Press, 1994.
Fritsch C. T. "'God Was with Him': A Theological Study of the Joseph Narrative," *Interpretation* 9 (1955), pp. 21–34.
Honeyman, A. M. "The Occasion of Joseph's Temptation: Gen 39:11ff.," *Vetus Testamentum* 2 (1952), pp. 85ff.
Jeansonne, Sharon Pace. *The Women of Genesis*. Minneapolis: Fortress Press, 1990.
Niditch, Susan. *Folklore and the Hebrew Bible*. Minneapolis: Fortress Press, 1993.
Redford, D. B. *A Study of the Biblical Story of Joseph (Gen. 37–50)*. Leiden: E. J. Brill, 1970.
Steinberg, Naomi. *Kinship and Marriage in Genesis*. Minneapolis: Fortress Press, 1993.
Von Rad, Gerhard. *Theology of the Old Testament*, volume 1. London: SCM Press, 1962, 1975.

Ward, W. A. "The Egyptian Office of Joseph," *Journal of Semitic Studies* 5 (1960), pp. 144–150.

Westermann, Claus. *Genesis: An Introduction.* Minneapolis: Fortress Press, 1991.

See also the bibliographies in C. Westermann, *Genesis 37–50* (Minneapolis: Fortress Press, 1986; London: SPCK, 1987).

Questions for Reflection

Chapter 1. The Peace Is Shattered in Jacob's Family (Genesis 37)
1. What was the significance in the world of Genesis of the father's favoring of one of his children?
2. What kinds of emotions among Jacob's family are described in Genesis 37?
3. Dreams have an important role in Genesis 37–50. What is the basic question in Joseph's dreams in this story?
4. What does the action of the oldest brother in Genesis 37 suggest about responsibility in our lives?
5. According to Genesis 37, what really makes a person a brother or sister?

Chapter 2. Joseph's Fall and Rise (Genesis 39:1–23)
1. What does this story suggest about God's presence in a foreign land?
2. What is the nature of the conflict faced by Joseph in relation to Potiphar's wife?
3. What does this story imply about God's protection of those who trust God? Can we expect to avoid tragedies in the short run? In the long run?
4. Do you think that human emotions, temptations, and anxieties are realistically portrayed in this story?

Chapter 3. Preparation for Joseph's Exaltation (Genesis 40:1–23)
1. What is the function of dreams in this story — and in Genesis 37–50 in general? How are they related to other forms of God's revelation?
2. Describe the roles of the baker and the butler in this story.
3. How are the actions of political authorities over individuals understood in this story?

Chapter 4. Joseph's Exaltation (Genesis 41:1–32)
1. Do you think that dreams do more than reveal a person's inner, often unconscious thoughts and feelings? What is the understanding of dreams in this story?
2. How can an announcement (like that of Joseph's to Pharaoh) function as a redemptive word in our lives?
3. Does this story shed any light on the proper interrelationships of (a) the political leaders, (b) the individual, and (c) God?

Chapter 5. Joseph's Exaltation and Duties in Egypt (Genesis 41:33–57)
1. How does our social context affect how we think? (In this story, compare the nomadic life of the Israelites with the cosmopolitan life of Pharaoh's court.)
2. How is "wisdom" understood in this story?
3. Is it appropriate to consider as gifts of God the abilities of persons who are administrators, economists, politicians, and other authorities in civil government?

Chapter 6. The First Journey of the Brothers to Egypt (Genesis 42)
1. What do you think Westermann means by the "inner" and the "outer" narrative lines?
2. In this story, the brothers must request food from foreigners. What personal dynamics are involved in the situation of requesting favors and granting them? What did Mother Teresa mean when she said that we would one day have to ask forgiveness from all those whom we have helped?
3. What elements of this story are different from social conditions today?
4. What are the good effects of the confession of sin?

Chapter 7. The Second Journey of the Brothers to Egypt (Genesis 43)
1. What is the significance of personal greetings in our society? In the world of Genesis 43?
2. What did eating together imply in the ancient Near East? Compare the practice in Genesis 43 with that of contemporary families.

3.   What can we learn about human relationships from the story of Genesis 43?

Chapter 8. The Silver Cup (Genesis 44)
1.   How do the legal proceedings of this story contrast with those of our time? What aspects of this story seem strange to you?
2.   How can Judah's behavior in this story serve as a model for us?
3.   How are sin and forgiveness related in this story? What can we learn from this about dealing with our own guilt?

Chapter 9. Joseph Reveals Himself and Offers Forgiveness (Genesis 45)
1.   What made forgiveness and reconciliation possible in this story?
2.   What does this story suggest about God's rule over human destiny?
3.   Is the moment of reconciliation presented realistically in this story?
     How common is such an experience in our lives?

Chapter 10. Jacob Blesses the Pharaoh (Genesis 47:7–10)
1.   What striking aspects and ironies can we find in the meeting of Jacob and Pharaoh?
2.   What is the significance of a humble person blessing one more powerful?
3.   What can we learn about human dignity from this story?

Chapter 11. Ultimate Forgiveness (Genesis 50:15–21)
1.   In what ways do these verses form the "true conclusion" of the story of Joseph?
2.   Read verse 20. How is it both an "assertion" and an "encouragement"? What does it suggest about how we can understand evil actions in our life and our society?
3.   Notice Westermann's comment on p. 109: "There is probably no other part of the Bible which speaks of God in such human terms." What part of the story of Joseph might he refer to with this comment?
4.   Which aspects of the story of Joseph can function as a guide to life today?